Lit Mag

Issues 1 & 2

KENESHA WILLIAMS, EDITOR-IN-CHIEF

DEDICATION

This is dedicated to all the Black women around the world.
You are wonderful and full of #blackgirlmagic

CONTENTS

ACKNOWLEDGMENTS

Thanks to Black Girl Magic Lit Mag's Co-editors:
Tiara Jante & Kortney Hinton

.

Issue 1

Letter from the Editor

Thank you for purchasing Black Girl Magic Lit Mag and supporting our mission.

Black Girl Magic Lit Mag is a literary magazine created to address the lack of diverse, non-majority voices and characters in speculative fiction, especially Black women's voices. Black Girl Magic Lit Mag believes that by showcasing stories featuring Black female voices and characters we can create a reflection of ourselves in the literature that we love, in a world where our images are constantly controlled, shaped, and distorted by those outside of our experiences.

We recognize all diverse experiences, including (but not limited to) QUILTBAG, people of color, gender diversity, people with disabilities, and ethnic, cultural, and religious minorities. Our mission is to increase visibility for diverse authors, specifically women of color, and empower a wide variety of readers in the process.

We sincerely hope you enjoy our first issue and that we will have many more to come! If you'd like to be kept up to date on what's happening with Black Girl Magic Lit Mag, speculative fiction book reviews, events, and news, consider subscribing to our newsletter https://tinyletter.com/blackgirlmagicmag

Best,
Kenesha Williams
Founder/Editor-in-Chief

Nautical Dawn - Miri Castor

The Gift of Twilight allows one to circumvent the forces that make the world what it is. A power as great as this will not stay with me forever, eventually I will perish and this Gift will be passed down to my descendants. I wish for many grandchildren, I can sense that my children will have many and that they will have many... I digress, this journal serves as a tool for my grandchildren and descendants. I can only hope that you will accept this Gift when you are presented with your truth, and live in this new world of Earth in peace. Our power is not a curse, but it is great. Great power can draw attention to those on the other side.

Opal Charm yawned as she slumped back on the sturdy couch. Shifting positions did nothing, the couch might as well have been a boulder. Ignoring the uncomfortable seat, Opal spoke her thoughts aloud, "The other side? He means this world."

On the insistence of her "friend", Adaeze Durgakama, Opal decided to venture to Athre today. Nothing was happening in her small home on Earth as far as she knew; she didn't have that much homework, and her parents would be coming home late. Her older sister, Sarah Charm, didn't care where Opal went after school and Opal wouldn't have it any other way.

She groaned as she tried to adjust herself snugly. She went back to reading the dinky book Addy told her to study, skipping a few pages with useless knowledge on Athre. She propped the book on her knees as her head reached the armrest; there was something peculiar about the handwriting and writing style on the sixth page.

Beatrix Charm. Grandfather kept telling me to add more pages to his book. His Twilight book for future Charms. He said I failed to see the understanding of it—his dying wish was for me to contribute, so...my Gift is time-

"Oooh, yes!" exclaimed Opal, sitting up in a jolt as she recognized her own Gift. She continued to read.

My Gift is time. I've grown up with it. I used it when I was younger. Wasn't sure what I was doing. Grandfather told that I had a dangerous Gift, that I could harm people and myself. I've—

Opal squinted at the yellowed page, trying to make out the inky words scribbled out by the author. She sucked her teeth as she turned the next page; as she attempted to read the illegible lines, she heard creaking by the rickety staircase. She looked up to see Adaeze, the deep sienna-skinned leader of Justice Allegiance for Every Lusan, staring at Opal curiously. Even after a few months of knowing her, Opal wasn't sure whether to be formal or casual. "H-hi Adaeze", greeted Opal nervously.

"Hello Opal," replied Adaeze with a faint smile. "Am I disturbing you?"

"No."

"Good". Adaeze's dark auburn eyes went to Opal's head. Opal was never sure how the Athrenian felt about her, there was a lot she didn't know about Adaeze. She used to think it was because she wasn't a human, but it didn't make sense— Athrenians acted pretty similar to humans. She always had that enigmatic air around her, ever since she recruited Opal into JAEL.

Wow, was it only a year ago?

Opal remembered when she wounded up in Athre and meeting Adaeze and Evron Moreno, the two founding members of JAEL. They thrusted a great responsibility on her when they told her of the nearly-immortal dictator that ruled all of Lusa's districts, and that she was currently the only person in her family that could defeat him before he found Earth. He had an incredible Gift called Lasondeké, some forbidden, "dark art" that had something to do with his partial immortality, and he would use it to kill people—Opal regurgitated the same things Adaeze would tell her, but never answered her other questions. What would he do if he found Earth? Why did her predecessor place a seal on him that ensured his death would be at the hands of a Charm? What was he gonna do if he ruled all of Athre? All were unresolved questions that were always in the back of Opal's mind.

Opal used to hate JAEL for everything—for giving her the task to kill someone she didn't even know, and for forcing her to face the parts of herself she pretended didn't exist in order to awaken her Gift. It was hard for Opal to see her Twilight as something that made her extraordinary when people-or Athrenians-merely saw it as a means to an end.

"You appear lost in thought", observed Adaeze sternly, leaning on the backrest of the sofa. Opal scooted back from her face as it was inches away from Opal's. Adaeze snorted. "Will you keep your hair in its natural state?"

Opal nodded, pulling on the springy, tight coils in the front of her hair. She missed playing with her hair when she had it pressed—it was flat and stiff. Now it was full of curly life.

Adaeze smiled with an approving nod.

It was a good thing Adaeze was smiling, otherwise Opal would have no idea on whether or not she was being sarcastic or not. Adaeze sighed as she walked around the couch, sitting next to Opal. Opal brought her knees to her chest as Adaeze sat up straight and stroked her long braids back. *Adaeze's has way more muscle in her legs than I do,* realized Opal, scrutinizing Adaeze's chubby thighs with some envy. Opal used to have bony arms that could barely lift a couple of textbooks. Now, there was some developed muscle in both her arms and legs, but Opal wished for more.

I'm still a twig.

"How are you with Randolph's book?" asked Adaeze briskly.

Opal cleared her throat. "I'm reading Beatrix's part. She said she had the Gift of time 'n that it was dangerous."

"Ah, that part."

"But it's all scribbled out. I dunno what the rest says," groaned Opal. "I'm pretty sure she time traveled, too. I wanna see how she did it."

Adaeze lowered her eyes before looking to Opal with a pensive look. The weak, pale sunlight fell on Adaeze's face, revealing the long scar from her brow to her nose. Opal refocused on her intense stare. "It is only fitting I show you," said Adaeze softly with a sigh.

"Huh?" Opal placed the book beside her.

Adaeze stood over Opal, gesturing for her to stand. "You need to be in a certain pose for it to work. A plethora of Twilight needs to flow from your hands and be centered. Here, I will help you position them."

"R-really?" Opal sprung to her feet and eagerly gave Adaeze her hands. "Wait, what's a plethora?"

Adaeze didn't raise her eyes from Opal's hands. "A lot."

She thought Adaeze wouldn't be too keen on the idea of Opal doing time travel. "Temperamental" or "volatile" was what Adaeze would've called it, that's what she always called Opal's Gift of Twilight. Opal was suddenly suspicious. "Wait, why're you helping me? How do you know how to do this anyway?"

"I've studied the concept of time. There are Athrenians that have this Gift", answered Adaeze matter-of-factly, opening up Opal's palms. "However, their Gift is different than your Twilight-enhanced temporal abilities. And why?" Adaeze chuckled, then sighed gloomily. "You wished to know. Now, you must position your arm like so."

Opal wondered if Adaeze was telling her the whole story. Along with that air of mystery, Opal had a feeling she wasn't ever getting the entire truth from her; Adaeze's instructions superimposed on whatever inklings of suspicion Opal had left. She lifted Opal's right hand over her left, then told her to bend her fingers. It was an uncomfortable position to hold as Adaeze began explaining the relevance of it. "This is called Primal Temporé. It allows you to jump backwards into the river of time, how far you go back depends on your power. Focus Twilight from your left arm, then cradle it with the Twilight from your right handle."

"Cradle it?" Opal bit down on her bottom lip. Her arms began to ache as she tried to imagine what Adaeze said. She shook her head with downcast eyes. "I don't think-"

"You can." Adaeze's tone closed off any kind of argument. "You've been training with Evron, you should be more than capable by now."

Opal closed her eyes and let out a soft breath. Warm Twilight pulsated from her chest, spreading with every heartbeat. She felt the warmth collect in her arms, now it was a matter of evening out the distribution of Twilight. A year ago, Opal couldn't imagine her life like this—going through her last year in junior high in a normal suburban town while training to become a powerful Twilight user in another world. *I was a loser. I hated everything and everyone because I was scared of losing them,* remembered Opal sadly, opening her eyes. *I'm not afraid anymore.*

A burst of gold erupted from Opal's palms. The sphere shone as bright as the sun, Opal couldn't help but grin. Opal's Twilight felt like summer's warmth, like the lazy days she spent locked away in her bedroom hating the world and playing ancient games on her flip phone. Opal wished for a better summer this year, a summer with her best friends at the beach, floating in the calm waters of Dewdrop Beach.

Opal could feel her Twilight fading, the whips of energy that nearly licked her and Adaeze's faces were weakening. The golden sphere vanished with a great enough force to shove Opal down to the floor. She remained stunned while disappointment settled on Adaeze's face. As Adaeze opened her mouth to comment, someone interjected behind Opal.

"What were you tryin' to do?" demanded Evron in surprise. She didn't know he was standing there all this time.

"It's none of your business", retorted Opal as she pushed herself up and brushed her hands on the bottom half of her navy blue jumper. Evron swept and mopped the floors every other day, but Opal still felt the need to keep her hands cleans.

"It is too!" snapped Evron excitedly. With a cocky sneer, he added, "I'm your teacher."

Opal groaned in disgust as she rolled her eyes. She hated thinking about it and she hated it even more when Evron used that excuse for everything. He was well-aware of it, too, which was why he shoved it in Opal's face all the damn time; it sucked that even though Opal was supposed to be the one with the omnipotent Gift, she was a novice. What sucked even more was that Evron was in charge of training her to be a Twilight user—he didn't even have Twilight as his Gift! "Warping the forces that governed space" as Adaeze put it, was his Gift and wasn't remotely related to Opal's Gift.

Besides, Evron basically hated her. He hated her before she joined JAEL, got a little bit nicer afterwards, and now Opal lived in the realm of his general exasperation and sincerity. *He barely cares about me too, everyone just cares about my Twilight.*

"Opal was attempting to utilize her temporal Gift," explained Adaeze, folding her muscular, big-boned arms.

The umber skinned boy gave Opal a look of bewilderment, then laughed scornfully. "There was no way you could manage that." He waved the possibility away. "No va pasar."

"What d'you know?" objected Opal, clearly offended. She could hear Adaeze laughing behind her darkly; Opal suddenly wished her best friend, Aaron Reyes, was here to support her. But he wouldn't be, and Opal couldn't figure out why. He barely spoke to her anymore—months after Opal joined JAEL, he was excited to accompany her to Athre and help JAEL in any way he could. Without him being the friendly buffer, being around Adaeze and Evron was awkward and taxing. "I probably could," grumbled Opal to the floor.

"I know what you can't and can do."

Opal's fists tightened. When Evron wasn't ordering her around and being oddly nice sometimes, he was being rude. *He'll come around after you start training with him,* Opal recalled Aaron's words bitterly.

He still hasn't!

"'Sides, isn't that time stuff complicated?" he asked Adaeze, his eyes narrowed. "Why are you lettin' her do this?"

Adaeze placed her hands behind her back, looking from Evron to Opal. "Because she can." Opal heard her resolute tone, Adaeze actually believed in her. "She is a Charm with the Gift of time. As her assigned mentor, wouldn't you hope she achieved the rare feat of manipulating time?"

Evron gnashed his teeth as he turned away, flustered. "N-not really."

"Oh?" In Adaeze's surprise, her tone remained flat.

"Why not? You don't think I'm strong enough?" asked Opal, fuming. "Jeez, you don't think I can do anything."

Adaeze watched Opal huff and stomp her bare foot on the fragile floor. She looked like she was observing the behavior of mice in cage. Evron turned around, his brows sharp.

"That's not-"

Opal turned to Adaeze in an angry huff with her hands raised, trying to remember how she positioned Opal's hands earlier. "Can you help me do this again?"

"In this state, you cannot. Whatever you conjure now will not be enough to sway Evron's opinion of you," replied Adaeze brusquely. Opal dropped her hands to her sides and sucked her teeth. "There is one thing you can do."

"What?" Opal stepped closer to Adaeze while exchanging a glare with Evron. He had his arms folded, also waiting for Adaeze's reply.

"You can prove yourself in a mock duel against him," stated Adaeze. Evron's jaw dropped while Opal gasped.

"Addy! There's no way—" protested Evron, stepping beside Opal. "I'm supposed to be showin' her stuff and doing light sparring. You even told me not to—"

"Fine," mumbled Opal scornfully. Adaeze knew Evron much longer than she had, she knew what would satisfy Evron and what wouldn't. Opal trusted in Adaeze's instincts, she was right about everything anyway.

"What?" Evron whipped his head to Opal, his braid-out bouncing a bit.

"Are you sure, Opal?" Adaeze patted Evron's shoulder with an amused smirk. "A mock duel in Athre requires you to go full force on each other. Evron understands this." She glanced at Evron, then chuckled. "You appear apprehensive."

Evron jumped back from her, stammering, "N-no! I'm not—I didn't hear her."

"Let's go then, *Teacher*," snapped Opal as she stepped towards him. Although Evron was set off by anything and had a temper, she found it easier to challenge him than some of the girls at school. Maybe it was because she got to know him better after joining JAEL, or because Adaeze basically told her Evron was all bark without any bite. "I'm tired of you talkin' down to me like I'm a stupid kid who doesn't know anything— you don't respect me! So let's go, you 'n me."

Evron furrowed his thick brows, flabbergasted at the challenge. His dark hazelnut eyes were casted to the floor for a moment. He muttered, "Do I—?"

Opal waited a second, then pulled back from the taciturn fourteen year old. "Do you what?"

He broke into a vigorous snicker that echoed in the dingy shack. While Opal wondered where that came from-Adaeze's amused expression couldn't provide Opal with any sort of clues-Evron shook his arms out and pulled the trapdoor open. "You wanted to go? Let's go."

Opal followed Evron and Adaeze down the dimly lit stairwell. No matter how many times she went down these steps, the narrow stairwell still felt claustrophobic to her. Opal began to wonder what she had gotten into. *This was a bad idea, I might've actually pissed Evron off,* thought Opal as she reached the platform at the bottom of the stairs.

Karimu, the humongous snake that's been owned by the Charm family since forever, was absent in the gaping, hollow chamber. Evron leaped in the pit eagerly while Adaeze sat at the ledge; they were both dressed like typical Athrenians. Evron had on a black shirt with straps of exposed Velcro around the sleeves and short harem pants, and Adaeze wore a black romper that made the crimson tint of her skin more noticeable. As if she felt Opal's hesitation, she turned around to her. "Are you beginning to regret this?"

"Y-yeah," admitted Opal, clutching the back of her head. Adaeze chuckled, as usual. "Are you sure he'll respect me if I do this?"

"No."

"Wha-what!?" Opal waited for a response, but Adaeze just stared. Opal raised her shoulders as her fists tightened. "That's my whole reason for doing this. And you're sayin' there's no point?"

"I jest," replied Adaeze nonchalantly. "I believe you will learn to respect one another by participating in this, by displaying the maximum strength of your Gifts."

"Er, okay," muttered Opal, relaxing her shoulders. "I guess I'll pull through."

"I will stop the duel if it gets out of hand."

Opal sighed. *A good luck would've been fine, too. I wish Aaron was here.* He would've been screaming his head off in sheer excitement. Maybe he could've stopped this, too—no, Aaron loved shit like this. Not her and Evron fighting, but both of them using their Gifts and "showing off". *He's ridiculous,* thought Opal with a smile.

Opal ran and hopped off the ledge and landed on her feet. She remained in a slightly crouched position with both her hands up. Evron raised his hands as well, smirking at Opal. Whatever reluctance he had before was gone, his stance was poised and aggressive. "You better be ready," warned Evron.

Opal glared at him and began concentrating on the Twilight within her. *Coat yourself with Twilight,* she reminded herself, a lesson from Evron. She couldn't hold back, she had remember that.

Neither of them moved until Adaeze shouted, "Begin".

Evron reacted first, conjuring a sharp, violet crescent with a quick hand swipe. Opal narrowly missed it as she jumped out of its way. It disappeared before reaching the other end of the chamber; she felt a breeze behind her when Opal landed on her feet. When she turned, Evron kicked her in the back and sent her tumbling to the floor. Opal rolled on her side and pushed herself up, shaking off the pain from the light kick.

Twilight gleamed in her palms as Opal lunged towards Evron, cocking both hands back. When she got in close to him, she aimed her punches for his face; her frustration grew as he moved accordingly, his expression remaining solemn. She expected him to be shouting or at least making her feel shitty about herself—he wasn't like this when they trained. He was really taking this seriously.

"Hands up!" barked Evron, back fisting Opal across the face. Evron's fist felt like a jagged stone, she knew this from training with him. Warm liquid welled up in her mouth; Opal spat some blood on the floor. The mixture of adrenaline and Twilight mitigated his blows, but they still hurt like hell. Without warning, Evron bent down and brandished his arms, summoning violet crescents that were aimed towards her. Opal amplified the golden Twilight in her hands and formed a sandy, dome shield in front of her. She slid inches back as Evron's spatial matter collided against her shield. *Always rush in after defending,* Opal remembered Evron's lesson. *But what if he's—*

Something strong blasted Opal's shield, bringing her to her knees. She winced as her backside and arms throbbed; even with the cover of Twilight, Evron's strength was shooting through her like a dozen needles shoved into her arms and back. He was holding back when he sparred with her. "You're supposed to be better than me," stated Evron as he walked up to a haggardly breathing Opal. Her head was to the floor as she everything around her grew dim. That was the last thing Opal expected to hear from someone like Evron. "You're so twiggy" and "You're hopeless", was what he said most of the time. Was this one of his random moments of sincerity that just popped up sometimes?

Evron shook his head with a disgruntled look. "You can't protect anyone like this."

Opal raised her head as she gawked at him, tears welling up in her eyes.

"No tiene sentido."

That was Evron's response to the answer Opal gave him. They were in the pit, Opal slumped against the wall in her jumper while coughing, panting, sweating, and trying not to faint. Evron worked her until she could barely stand. She wiped the sweat from her eyes, then dug her nails into her curly updo. "Wha?" gasped Opal. "English...por...favor."

Evron dropped his arms to his sides exasperatedly. "Why don't you learn Spanish?"

Opal sighed. "I am."

"Like actually learn it 'stead of sitting in a forty minute class goin' over verb conjugations. Ay dios mio." He rubbed his temple. "I said that doesn't make sense."

Opal shook her head and with a vexed tone asked, "Whaddya mean it doesn't make sense? I don't need some dumb reason to fight—I just do it."

"Eso te hace una maníaca," replied Evron with a grimace, shaking his head. "You're a psycho. A freak."

"So what if I am!?" griped Opal, resting her head on her knees. "What're you fighting for? What kind of weird question is that? You guys just need me to fight so I can kill Samael. So that's what I'll do."

She heard his flat footsteps grow nearer, and then felt him beside her. He sighed through what sounded like his nostrils. "You...you love your parents, right?"

Opal was taken aback. She had to look at him to make sure he wasn't being a dick or something. He was glaring at her, but he didn't seem mad.

"Yeah," replied Opal timidly.

"A-Aaron too, yeah?" stammered Evron. He was probably remembering when he had awkwardly asked her and Aaron if they were going out. "I-I mean, you care 'bout him. Not like that, but like—you know."

Opal nodded. She was starting to see what he was getting at, despite fumbling over his words. "I care about all of them," affirmed Opal. It was funny, she had spent the past three years of her life trying to deny any feelings towards her friends and family. She was afraid to love them because she was a coward—she didn't want to lose any of them like she lost her big brother, Jermaine. And now, I can't stop saying it, *thought Opal*. "That's why I have to learn how to fight. So I can to protect them."

"Gettin' a valid reason to fight is a start," said Evron, his expression and tone softening. Opal looked at him, realizing what he had helped her realize. She was nothing without them, her parents, her siblings, her friends—they were everything that Opal wanted to keep safe. What was the point of Gifts and Twilight if she couldn't protect them?

"Thanks Evron," said Opal warmly.

He stepped back, his fingers twitching. Opal noticed his cheeks were a bit flushed, she smiled weakly. "You're blushing? Didn't know you could do that."

"Ai, noestoysonrojando!"

"What?"

"B-back to—let's...break time's over!"

Opal wiped her eyes and felt Twilight surge through her body, giving her the strength to stand. "You're right," admitted Opal.

Beating Evron right here would prove everything—it would prove that she could protect those precious to her, that she could defeat Samael, and that she was more than capable of achieving her "maximum strength". Opal screamed as she lunged towards Evron, her fists shining as she held two miniature suns in her palms. He was focused on the Twilight spheres, and not on her feet; she jumped backwards and then thrusted her fists out towards him. *Please, let it work this time. Please...*

The golden sand from her knuckles quickly formed a pair of colossal hands that punched Evron as he was preparing to form another spatial crescent. When Opal stumbled onto her feet, she saw Evron lying in a small crater in the wall. He groaned as he fell forward, but then caught himself as he hovered above the ground. Evron was drastically altering gravity, as a part of his Gift; as he slowly descended, he unleashed a flurry of stationary kicks. He would've looked really stupid if he hadn't formed more crescents with those kicks; Opal ducked under one, jumped over the other, and sprinted towards him. He dropped to the floor and sliced the air with a knife hand slash.

Opal cocked her right arm back, the respective fist followed suit. She sent her massive, golden fist into the spatial matter. It cut through the sandy knuckles, but Opal's fist managed to destroy it, releasing a gust of purple air that clouded her vision. It didn't matter, Evron didn't move from where he was; she saw his silhouette in front of her. Through the turbulent wind, she jabbed at him, sending the huge, crumbling fist into him.

When she was sure she got him, she allowed herself to fall on her knees. That was the first time she was able to use two fists at once, Opal amazed herself. *Is this my maximum strength?*

She looked up to see Evron slumped against the wall, breathing wretchedly. He was struggling to keep his eyes open, it looked like he was done. Then he held his palm out, Opal anticipated another spatial crescent.

Opal cried out as pain broke through her inner Twilight covering; she pushed herself up clumsily as she panted, cocking her unsteady arm back. *I won't lose, I can't lose,* chanted Opal silently.

"We're done."

Opal stopped, lowering her arm as she looked to Adaeze. She was now in the pit with the two of them, approaching Opal with an amused expression. "And here I thought I had to watch out for you. Nice job Opal." She bowed her head a little, then turned to Evron. "Despite the outcome, Opal still needs your guidance."

"You-you sure?" groaned Evron, rubbing his swollen cheek.

"Really?" whined Opal in between breaths, hunched over to lean on her knees. She had hoped winning this duel proved to herself and Adaeze that she didn't need anyone to treat her like a stupid kid anymore. "So that wasn't my maximum strength?"

Adaeze smiled at her. "That was nowhere near it." Her smile fell as she looked to Evron. "Much of her strength is misplaced. Please see to that."

She looked down at Opal, gripped her aching shoulder, and fascinatedly gazed into her eyes, as if trying to find something within them. With a satisfied smirk, she released Opal's shoulder and went to the steps embedded in the wall, returning to the upper platform. Hearing Evron's groan brought Opal's attention back to him.

"You're gonna be fine, right?" asked Opal haughtily, too proud to give him a hand. He nodded as he clutched his drooping head. She began to worry. "H-hey…"

"You always…had my…respect…Opal," muttered Evron softly. "I'm sorry. We didn't…need to…do this."

Opal covered her agape mouth, turning away. She was flustered and always shocked by how sincere he could be sometimes. She didn't know how to respond; she sighed exhaustedly as she dropped on her back, staring up at the tall ceiling. She stretched her arms and legs out, and then closed her eyes. Almost immediately, she heard Evron barking at her, "Hey, wake up! We have more work to do, we're not done today."

Opal groaned, opening her eyes to see him standing over her. "I wasn't sleeping."

"It got easier when you remembered why you're fighting, yeah?"

Evron held his hand out. Opal weakly smiled back, gripping his hand. Even if Aaron was mad at her, or if her parents were disappointed in her, they were precious to her. Jermaine, Anza, Adaeze, and Evron were important, too. She wouldn't lose any of them to Samael and his Gift, or whatever Athre would throw at them.

"Yeah."

Interview with Miri Castor

What was your inspiration for this story?

My own imagination, I guess? Superficially speaking, this story was based off my planned sequel to my first novel Opal Charm: The Path to Dawn. On a deeper level, I was inspired by my video games.

Why did you choose a black woman for your main character?

I love my RPGs, fantastical video games, and my speculative fiction books. However, they all lack main characters that look like me. Black girls in fiction are either invisible or jaded stereotypes. My ultimate dream is to have a black girl be all-loving superhero that everyone adores, the chosen one, and all of the above. White children have plenty of those. If I had a black girl superhero in my childhood, my self-esteem when I was younger would've been higher.

Why did you want to submit to Black Girl Magic Lit Magazine?

It fits with my ultimate dream. Nothing's better than magical black girls.

What are your favorite novels or short stories and why?

Favorites are Kindred by Octavia Butler, and A Storm of Swords by George Martin. Kindred comes closest to my ideal science fiction--a black female main character who time travels. A Storm of Swords was just the best book in A Song of Ice and Fire series--and the craziest.

Tell us something about your future writing projects.

I hope to have many future writing plans! I'm publishing my debut novel Opal Charm: The Path to Dawn later this winter, possibly early spring. I hope to get started on the sequel story soon. You're kind of getting a glimpse of what that sequel will be like.

You can find Miri on the following social media platforms:
http://miricastor.tumblr.com/
https://twitter.com/charmedcastor
https://facebook.com/charmedopal
https://wattpad.com/user/miricastor

Bang and a Whimper - Satya T Nelms

People used to take from the Earth without thinking about the balance they were disrupting. Even the ones who cautioned that the human race was standing on the precipice of destruction wore blinders. Each of them so sure that their theory of how it would all end, was the theory, but they were all wrong…and all right I suppose.

It started slow. In the parts of the country that still had some semblance of seasons, the summers got hotter, then the springs. The Southern states became intolerable in the summer time, and barely live-able the rest of the year. The better portion of California was either under water or wiped out from drought and fires.

The Pacific Northwest and New England became prime real estate. This caused the Second Great Migration, and beginnings of the civil wars that would soon follow as millions of the displaced made their way North.

Then Methanobacterium Crimea Virus (MCV) hit. At first everyone thought it was a strong strain of flu, but as people started dying first by the hundreds, and soon by the thousands, whole towns started being held under quarantine. The infection spread like wildfire throughout the world for half a decade, and when it was finally over, only a third of the world's population was left. We were referred to as The Immune.

The world that remained after all of that was nothing like the world before. The abundance of generations past was gone. Humanity was reduced to base instinct. The power hungry fought to carve out their own dominions in the new world. The people occupying their chosen region could only hope that their overlord would be a benevolent one, although it was best not to get attached as assassinations and coups were a monthly, sometimes weekly occurrence.

The remnants of the government struggled to regain control. Soldiers were sent to the remaining cities to maintain order. Curfews were imposed. Resources were rationed. But there simply weren't enough soldiers to go around, and those who had gotten a taste of power were not keen to give it up. They called themself the Fringe.

When they arrived in Boston, they swept the area, looting where they could and enslaving those they could catch. I'd been living on my own in the Outerlands for close to two years when the caught me. I grew what food I could, surviving on the crops and rations I'd managed to bring with me when I fled. Those lasted well over a year, but after that I had to make monthly trips into the city for supplies.

Two Fringe soldiers caught me leaving an abandoned home in a residential neighborhood the morning I was captured. I braced myself to run, but they raised their guns and I knew I would either be taken or killed. I chose the former.

We marched into the center of the city and everything was gray. The sky. The garbage littering the empty streets. It looked as though any remaining life that hadn't been taken by disease or poverty had been taken by The Fringe, and with that life had gone all of the color. We approached what used to be a low-income housing development. A swing on the playground at the center of the development creaked in the wind, singing a sorrowful song in the absence of a child to enjoy it.

The lights in the hallway flickered and I gagged on the odor of insufficient sanitation. Bringing my feet up from the floor required extra effort as they briefly adhered to the mystery coating on the stairs. On each landing there was an armed man guarding the door to the floor behind him. As we kept ascending the stairs I would hear an occasional scream, usually followed by a callous cackle.

I lost track of how many flights we'd walked but looked up when we stopped walking to discover there were no more flights left. We walked down all the way to the end of the hall until we came to the last apartment on the right. A handful of women were huddled in the corner of the living room farthest from the entryway. There was a soiled mattress in the center of the room, and all the windows had been blocked out.

In truth, that corner was filled with women and girls. The youngest couldn't have been a day over 14, and the oldest... The oldest was hard to peg. I suspected whatever had gone on in this room aged the women beyond the usual passage of time. It's funny how trauma can do that.

Once the door closed behind me the huddled mass seemed to take a collective breathe. The women began to disperse around the room. One of the older ones took me by the elbow. There were dark hollows under her eyes carved into her olive skin and she wore a long gray garment.

She guided me down a hallway to my right. We stopped at the second door to the left.

"That's the bathroom," she said.

We took another two steps and she stopped at a door next door to the bathroom.

"This is your room", she pointed toward the door.

She turned to walk back toward the living room.

"Wait," I said to her. "What's your name? Who's in charge? How long have you been here?"

The woman kept walking down the hall like she hadn't heard me.

While I'd been watching the older woman walk down the hall, the door she'd indicated as mine had opened. A short woman, 30, maybe 35 years old with tan skin, almond eyes, and curves that could still be detected even underneath the shapeless garb she wore stood in the entryway, talking to me.

"Don't take it personally." she said

"Who are you?" I asked her.

"Jules," she said. "You?"

"Maia." I looked down the hall and gestured in the direction of the woman who had brought me here.

"Who's she?" I asked Jules.

"Miranda," Jules said. "She's one of the originals."

"The originals?"

Jules let out a deep sigh. "Where you from newbie?"

"The Outerlands."

"Really? Don't think we've ever gotten anyone from out there before. How long were you out there?"

"Couple years."

"Hmm. Well, a lot has changed since you've been gone."

"I saw that."

She pushed the door open wider behind her. "Why don't you come in and have a seat, so I can catch you up."

Jules walked me through the room that would be my home for years to come, though I didn't know it yet. The paint on the walls was peeling in big ugly patches. Splintered beige gave way to an institutional gray in the parts that hadn't been stripped completely. The closet doors had been removed to make more room for bodies, and just like in the living room, the windows had been blacked out with what looked to be industrial strength paint.

"Why'd they do that to the windows?" I asked Jules.

"I think it's a control thing. They tell us when it's day, they tell us when it's night. They tell us when to eat. They tell us when we can wash—"

"When you can go outside", I tried to fill in the blanks for her.

"No. We never go outside." Jules words sounded ominous but she said them as if in passing.

We walked down the middle of heaps of blankets organized to designate the boundaries of each inhabitants' personal space. Jules stopped toward the middle.

"This is me." She pointed down at the nearest palette on the floor. "You can take the one next to me. She's not here anymore."

"Where did she go?" I asked.

Jules ignored my question, and moved on with her own. "So, were you here when the Fringe got here?"

"I left the day they came."

"Hmph. Lucky."

"None of us knew how many of them there were. You know, the government always downplayed them. Tried to make it seem like they weren't really a threat, but there were thousands of them when they came."

"Thousands?"

"Yeah. First they stormed Cambridge and then they marched right over Longfellow Bridge. They looted any shops that had managed to stay open, and when they were done with them they burned them down. They burned half the city to the ground."

"What about the police?"

Jules chuckled bitterly. "The police were useless. There just weren't enough of them. Most of them were killed, and the ones that weren't either managed to escape or surrendered."

"How long did all of this take?"

"The city was under Fringe control within a week."

"Jesus."

"Yup. The people that are in this building, and I'm guessing the ones around it, are the ones who either were caught in the original sweeps, or got found later on at some point."

"What are the sweeps? What do you mean got found?"

"When the people started fleeing, and trying to go into hiding, they started sweeping the area block by block. Sniffing folks out, and dragging them back to their compound. Most people here were caught in the beginning, but some of them are the stragglers. The ones who thought they wouldn't be found. Who holed up in apartments way over in the Southend thinking they were out of the Fringe's reach, but nobody is out of their reach."

"And what do they do with all of them – I mean us?"

"They break us and eventually convert us. How do you think their numbers keeping growing?"

I shook my head in disbelief, but Jules kept going.

"The higher floor you're on, the lower you are on the totem pole. And as you can see we're on the very top floor. I've been here for over a year, and I've only seen one person transferred."

"How do you get transferred?"

"You survive, I guess."

"Survive what?"

Jules looked away from me and chewed the inside of her cheek, but wouldn't answer.

It started as psychological warfare. I woke in the middle of the night to find a Fringe soldier watching me. Sometimes he was sitting on the end of my bed. Other times he was sitting on the bed next to me. Once I woke and he was lying on my palette, his face inches from mine. Smiling. I slept fitfully, waking often, fearful of where I would find him next.

At first I didn't say anything about him to Jules, but after a week of his appearances, I had to. I asked her why he was looking at me, and all she said was "Be grateful all he's doing is looking". I didn't feel very grateful, but I also didn't know what was coming.

Waking hours were passed in monotony. The women were all in various stages of unraveling, depending on how long they'd been there, and their coping mechanism of choice. Some sat talking to themselves in the corners, too broken to ever be built back up. Some preyed on the weak ones, satisfying their need to have some semblance of control over something in their lives. Others made an effort to develop a routine, no matter how basic or mundane. Jules was one of these, and I tried to follow her lead.

After I'd been on the top floor for a month, my visitor stopped coming in the night. After a week I began to start sleeping normally again, no longer concerned about who might be there when I woke. Two weeks later, rough hands woke me up in the night. They pulled me to my feet before my eyes had a chance to fully open. I squinted and noted that all of the other beds in the room were empty. When I shuffled into the living room I understood why.

All of the women from my room were standing in a circle around the soiled mattress in the middle of the floor. Everyone looked at their feet. I searched frantically for Jules, but couldn't make her out amidst the bodies. That was the first time I looked at the body that belonged to the rough hands. It was my visitor, and he was smiling again. He led me toward the mattress, and I knew what was coming.

I let my body go limp, hoping my dead weight would encumber his efforts, but he was determined. I fought. I squirmed. I spat at him. But it only seemed to enhance the experience for him. I clenched my thighs and my jaw together, but he pried them apart. Nothing I did to counter him was of any consequence. He took me anyway, while the circle of women stood by and watched.

The next morning I sought Jules out. "Did you know that would happen to me?"

She refused to look at me. I grabbed her by her shoulders and asked her again, even though she refused to meet my eyes. "Did you know that would happen to me?" Still nothing.

"Why wouldn't you have warned me? Why wouldn't you have said something?"

Still looking at anything but my face, she spoke, "Nothing I said would have changed anything. Mason takes what he wants", and then she jerked my hands off her and walked away.

I couldn't help but feel that every person I saw was complicit in what had happened to me. When I looked into their faces, all I saw was their knowing and it isolated me. When I was shown simple kindness, I thought it was somehow meant to compensate for what had been done and I rejected it. When the women bowed their heads in my presence and kept their distance, I perceived it as an admission of guilt and I looked at them with disgust. Even when I was treated brusquely or rudely, in my mind they were trying to force me past the incident, so I held them in contempt. I wore my distrust like an impermeable shroud and for a little while my indignation kept me alive. I would never become what these women had become. I would never treat another the way these people had treated me. I would die first.

This is what I told myself in the days and weeks that followed my brutal initiation into life with the Fringe. I ate alone. I spoke to no one. I moved my palette to a corner and faced the wall when I slept. Any time someone tried to strike up a conversation, I kept moving past them as though they had never uttered a word. This was how I would ensure my survival, I thought, by living apart, by not allowing the complacency and indifference that plagued these other women to infect my mind. If Calliope hadn't come, I don't know what would have happened to me.

New arrivals were few and far in between. A new woman would be brought in one day, another a few days later, and then no one for months. I had stopped counting time when the new girl who would be my successor arrived. Deeply absorbed in my mind at the time, it is a wonder I even noticed her, but her voice stood out amongst the others: high, frightened, questioning.

I raised my chin to identify the source of the sound, and then I saw her. Long, pin straight, black hair. Large oval eyes with delicate features besides, and skin the color of raw hazelnuts. No more than 15. The other residents of the top floor moved about her like she was invisible, obstinate in their determination not to acknowledge her. Her head swung wildly from one side to the other, her chest rising and falling in an erratic rhythm.

And then one of the women parted the sea of bodies, making her way toward the new captive. I squinted my eyes wondering who had decided to approach the fledgling and flew into a rage. Jules. I wrenched myself up from where I was sitting and strode across the floor. I shoved Jules to the side and pierced her with my glare.

"Stay away from her." I told her.

My sudden aggression seemed to shock her, but as she slunk away back into the shadows, I thought I heard her mutter "Good luck". I relaxed my shoulders, softened my jaw, and approached the girl slowly. I offered her half a smile.

"Hi, my name is Maia."

"Hi, I'm Calliope", she replied, cautious.

I reached out my arm and wrapped it around her shoulders while maintaining eye contact. I guided her to the room we would share, so I could tell her all that I had learned about this place where we had come to be, but would never call home.

When the Fringe arrived in Boston, Calliope was just a few months shy of her twelfth birthday. She lived with her mother Marie, never having known her father. Marie was only 16 when she had Calliope, which made them something less than mother and daughter, but something more than friends.

They lived in a one-bedroom apartment where Marie took the bedroom, and the living room space was split between Calliope and an area to entertain guests they seldom had. The local public school Calliope had attended shut down the year before the Fringe came due to lack of funding. Months after the school had stopped paying the teachers' salaries, they stopped being able to pay for the electricity, heat, and the last nail in the coffin- water.

A few of the parents from Calliope's grade level developed a home-schooling co-op of sorts. Three or four parents selected specific subjects to teach-history, math, literature, writing- and the others agreed to take on occasional special lessons, or provide lunches on a rotating schedule. Fifteen kids including Calliope made up this mobile school. They trekked together from one apartment building to another, all within a five-block radius, shuffling from class to class.

Calliope was in Mrs. Jenkins apartment discussing the finer points of Octavia Butler's Parable of the Sower when the screaming started in the streets. The screams were followed by the sound of hordes of feet slapping against the pavement. Mrs. Jenkins stopped mid-sentence, smiled to cover her worry, and told the students to write a reflection on how they thought the world might be different if people could feel the pain they inflicted on others. Then she rose from her chair, and walked with deliberate nonchalance to the window. She opened the blinds a crack, and her eyes grew wide. She stepped away from the window, and turned her back on what she saw.

She opened her mouth to speak and closed it again several times before she actually managed to get the words out. She smiled in a way that was too forced to be comforting and said, "Hey guys, I completely forgot we had a field trip scheduled for today, so I need everyone to pack up so we can head out. Quickly now, we're already late."

Calliope and all the other students looked into each other's faces, but didn't move from their seats. Sam designated himself to speak, since after all it was his mother. "What's going on?" he asked.

Mrs. Jenkins' eyes were pleading. She pursed her lips together, the last traces of her composure fading away, and then she said, "Quickly".

The students threw their bags onto their backs, and Mrs. Jenkins herded them out into the hallway. They moved through the building, down the stairwell and out onto the street below like a single many-legged being, stopping each time Mrs. Jenkins held up her hand, moving forward only when she indicated it was safe to do so. They were all silent but for the sounds of their shuffling feet, and the shifting of backpacks.

Outside on the street, people ran by them without seeing them, random items clutched to their chest – canned food, bundles of clothes, shoes, assorted books -- each person clinging to their own version of survival. Gaping holes stared out at them from storefronts that had managed to stay afloat. Boards had been pulled back from establishments that had long since been closed, as desperation drove people to leave no stone unturned.

Glass crunched underneath Calliope's feet as she huddled closer to her classmates. Smoke hung in the air as fires caught and spread from building to building. The sound of gunshots rang out through the air in the distance where the fire looked to have originated. Rather than walk away from all of that, they walked toward it. Soon the heat would be palpable on their skin; soon they may catch a glimpse of the owners of those guns. They had learned about this in History and Civil Studies with Mr. Davis. This was one of The Fringe's tactics. Herding. People's natural instinct was to run away from what they were walking into. So, the Fringe strategically placed their fires and their soldiers in key formations to funnel the population into areas where it would be easiest to sort them. More than half would be culled. Others would be absorbed into the Fringe, and though no one knew entirely what that meant, it was presented as the worst possible option.

So, Mrs. Jenkins pushed them through the throngs of people rushing in the opposite direction. Occasionally pulling them into alley-ways to walk side streets and in narrow spaces between buildings, so as not to attract unwanted attention to their little group. They were heading for a church basement just 7 blocks from where they'd come from. They'd taken various routes on a weekly basis, running this drill in lieu of The Fringe's inevitable arrival, but never had the walk felt so long.

They came out from behind an old, boarded-up warehouse back out onto the main street just one block from New Bethlehem African Methodist Episcopal Church, and two blocks from Calliope's apartment building, when she saw it. Her building – her apartment in particular – up in flames. Months of drills left her. Survival lessons painstakingly doled out over years of schooling were gone in an instant. She broke from the pack and took off toward her building, sure that she could hear the sound of her mother's screams over the deafening sounds of chaos on all sides of her.

Jeremy, a boy she'd known since kindergarten, caught her around the waist and yanked her backwards. Once back in the safety of their cluster he lifted her from the ground pinning her arms to either side of her body while Lucy restrained her thrashing legs. They held her this way for the remainder of the walk to the church making no efforts to gag her or muffle her cries which merely blended in to the other sounds around them.

Mrs. Jenkins ushered them to the back of the church, through a secret door behind a book case, and down a second hidden door in the floor beneath a dusty old rug, into a basement with no windows and a single door, where other members from the school community waited. Calliope's mother was not there. Her classmates and parents turned teachers turned guardians took turns standing in front of the door like sentries, obstructing her way to the outside. She fought them for hours, before finally crumpling into a ball in fits of tears on the floor and descending into a restless sleep.

She woke unsure if it was night or day, and surveyed the cots laid out in neat rows on the floor. She leaned in close to inspect a woman with dark curly hair on the far right of the room, but it wasn't her mother. She wasn't here, and somehow Calliope knew she never would be.

Stragglers continued to flood Calliope's basement refuge over the next 24 hours, then slowed to a trickle for the next few days and finally came to a halt at the end of the week. They had hidden out in empty apartments and abandoned cars slowly making their way there. All things totaled, they were 37. All crammed into that basement, with cots covering almost every inch of floor, no running water, and two toilets with bedpans where the bowl should be that had to be dumped strategically every 48 hours so as not to draw attention to their origins.

Some of her fellow classmates would pop up each time the door swung open, still hopeful that their missing parents, siblings, or friends had made it, and eager for news of the outside, but Calliope did not share their optimism or their fascinations with what was going on in the world. While the others held on to hope that just because their people hadn't made it to the church didn't mean they were dead – or worse – Calliope wore her pessimism like a shroud. The only world that existed for her was the world within the 4 walls of that windowless basement. As far as she was concerned, the only people left on the whole planet, were down there with her, but now that life had given her such a harsh lesson in impermanence, she would only allow herself to be so close to even them.

At first the adults forbade anyone under the age of 16 to make rounds – scouting out the area in strategic loops, looking for supplies – but the children far outnumbered them. The handful of adults could not support the dozens of occupants alone. So they began taking out the oldest of them one at a time – one youth for two adults. They did this until every adolescent over the age of ten had had a rotation outside, and were trained in the basics of how to conduct a run. After that adults were paired with the young ones, and a schedule was created.

Every couple of weeks Calliope emerged from the basement, cautious but calm. After a few months she even began to enjoy her brief stints outside – the feel of the sun on her face, the smell of the rain soaked pavement, the sounds of branches swaying in the wind. It was good to get out of that basement. After six months of relative peace, they all began to relax. The adults decided The Fringe was done sweeping their neighborhood for resources, and as long as they were careful, there could be no harm in letting people out in larger groups and extending the length of the runs.

The Fringe may have noticed them out before, and only been biding their time, or it's possible that that day's group was just unlucky, but on the first day exercising their new lax policy, no one made it back. Mrs. Jenkins, Sam, Abby, and two other adults Calliope had only met after coming to live in the basement, were all gone.

No one was allowed out for weeks after that. They rationed out the food and water even more strictly than usual, and dumped the human waste into a sealed trashcan that only slightly contained the smell. No one dared to speak above a whisper, and most of the time they all walked on the balls of their feet, afraid to let their heels make contact with the ground. For weeks they waited like this. Waited for one of the captured to crack and give them up. Waited for The Fringe to trace them back where they had come from. They didn't come, but life was never the same.

When they finally started going back out to restock dwindling supplies, they reverted back to only letting the adults out. There were five, maybe six of them left, so they struggled to move quickly and quietly while shouldering food, water, first aid and other miscellaneous goods for the rest of us, but they did it, and it was over a year before Calliope saw the outside again.

It was on her second or third run that she was caught. Without realizing it, Calliope's people and the Fringe had been dancing around each other for months. The Fringe had exhausted the resources in their immediate area, and Calliope's people had done the same with their neighborhood. So both parties began slowly widening their perimeter, until, without realizing it, those perimeters touched. The Fringe weren't out hunting people the day they found Calliope and the two male adults accompanying her, but stumbling upon them was a bonus prize.

I asked Calliope if she tried to run when they caught her; if she was scared.

She said, "Run back to what? To that half-life I'd been living for years in the basement? No, I didn't run. And I wasn't afraid. A part of me knew it would happen one day. Knew they would come for me. Knew I would be taken. It was only a matter of when. I was prepared for that moment every time I stepped outside."

I told her everything. I spared Calliope no details. She was young, but after listening to her story, I just knew she could handle it. She had to know what was coming. I would not have her blind-sided the way that I had been. I would not dance around the truth as Jules had done with me. I couldn't tell her everything all out in the open with the others watching and the guards making sporadic visits, so I told her in bursts.

I waited for her reaction; for her to say something, shed a tear, wring her hands, anything. But she never gave anything away. Occasionally while I was speaking she would chew on the corner of her lip, but other than that you would never have known what I was telling her from the look on her face. It was the same when she told me about herself. No bursts of emotion, no shudders at the remembrance of pain and anguish. She was always very matter of fact, she rattled off the story of her life's most pivotal years as if they had happened to someone else.

I asked her if she heard me, just to be sure, but a brief nod was all I got in response. I decided she was just processing all I had said – that she was grateful for the information and deciding how best to proceed. The last image I remember before falling asleep is her laying there on the floor, eyes open and unblinking, so still her features looked as though they may have been cast from clay.

When I woke up she had already left the room. We crossed paths as she was exiting the bathroom and I was entering. She gave me a small smile. I squeezed her hand as I passed. I found her sitting on the floor with the others, with an empty spot beside her that I would soon occupy, waiting for the guards to bring the morning's rations.

The sound of bolts being released, and locks springing open preceded the rattle of the doorknob. The guard entered balancing breakfast in one hand, while pushing the door open with the other. He was not one I recognized before; he looked young and eager to prove himself. He did not make eye contact with any of us, as he re-secured the door from which he had just come and strode into the center of the room where he placed soft Styrofoam containers on the floor. He pulled some napkins out of his back pocket, but no utensils. While I did not have overwhelming confidence in the intelligence of The Fringe, they were smart enough at least to know better than that.

As he turned to leave the way he had come, Calliope looked over at me, and placed one hand over mine. She gave me another smile, and then she got up and rushed the guard as he stood unlocking the door. She jumped on his back and slapped her hands against the side of his head, thrashing wildly. She appeared to be getting the better of him for a moment, but it must have only been the element of surprise because moments later he threw her down onto the floor. She flipped onto her belly, dove forward, and wrapped herself around his ankles, planting him to a spot just out of reach of the door. The guard jerked his hips from side to side trying to shake her off, but she wouldn't let go.

The guard seemed to remember his voice then and began shouting for her to release him. He bent over and began to pry her fingers from the death grip they had on him. I saw Calliope's fingers start to slip, and seemed to notice this too, because at that exact moment, she opened her mouth and bit down hard into the guard's fingers. He screamed, as the shock of the pain gave him a jolt of energy allowing him to wrench one of his legs from her grasp. He kicked her, hard, in the face, and flew backward.

Up until that point I had stood frozen in the spot Calliope had left me, watching her assault on the guard in slow motion, but unable to will myself to intervene. When I looked up and saw the blood pouring from her nose where the guards boot had connected, I got up and ran to the center of the room to shield her with my body. The guard was staring down at her with raw rage dripping from every pore. I heard the pounding of booted feet in the hallway and so did Calliope. She threw me off of her as the new guard's reinforcements stormed the room. Calliope surged forward, and without a second's hesitation, they pulled their guns holstered in the back of their pants, and shot her. Her body pulsed in the air as each bullet connected before slumping to the floor.

I dragged myself toward her, and lay my face beside hers as the light began to leave her eyes. As her last breaths shuddered in her breast, I whispered to her.

"Why did you do it?"

She smiled weakly at me. "I didn't want to wait anymore." She picked up her hand, battered and covered in blood, placed it on my cheek and closed her eyes. The guards removed her swiftly, and I remained there with only her blood on my face as a memento of her time together. I sat there and willed the tears to come, but they would not. Something inside of me seemed broken. I had reached my grief threshold. Though I was sad about what had happened to Calliope, I was unable to mourn her.

When I finally got up from the floor, an unlikely candidate stood before me. Jules. I look into her eyes, and said, "I killed her."

"How do you figure that?" she asked me.

"She did all of that on purpose. She knew what would happen. I told her what was coming. I told her what Mason would do, and this is what happened."

"She made that choice."

"I thought I was helping her."

"And I thought I was helping you."

She handed me a bit of breakfast she had set aside for me and walked away. She was right. My telling Calliope what would happen here had served her no better than Jules not telling me. This place had damned us all. I placed the breakfast Jules had given me on the floor, and made my way to our sleeping room. I sat down on my palette and contemplated how I would get out of there.

I studied the windows and the doors. I went into the bathroom and considered climbing out the window. I paced around that tiny little apartment with singular focus. To get out.

Interview with Satya Tara Nelms

What was your inspiration for this story?

I once heard that you should write the stories you want to read, and I love reading dystopian literature. I get lost in stories about alternative presents, and not too distant futures. However, whenever I read those stories, they usually seem to take place after the collapse of society has already happened. I wanted to read a story about someone living through the collapse. I wanted to have that experience through their eyes. So, I decided to write it.

Why did you choose a black woman for your main character?

My instinctual reaction to this question was, because I'm a Black woman, and though I think that is the answer in its simplest form, it is still true. My main character is a Black woman, because I am a Black woman, and I wanted to see a woman like myself, and like many of the women in my life that I know, love, and respect reflected in this character's journey.

Why did you want to submit to Black Girl Magic Lit Magazine?

The name of the magazine immediately caught my attention. There are lots of damaging stereotypes and words associated with Black girlhood and womanhood, so it was refreshing and affirming to see it associated with magic. Once I learned more about the magazine, I was even more excited. Octavia Butler is my most favorite author of all time, and it was while reading her work that I developed my love of speculative/science fiction. So, submitting to BGM Lit Magazine felt like a natural thing to do.

What are your favorite novels or short stories and why?

I have 3 children and choosing a favorite novel feels a bit like choosing a favorite child, but I if I just go with the first books that came to mind when I read the question, they would be: Parable of the Sower, by Octavia Butler and God Help the Child by Toni Morrison. Reading Parable of the Sower was a life-changing experience for me, so much so that I read it at least once a year. It changed the way I look at the world, and even my perception of God. Much like Octavia Butler, I don't think there is anything Toni Morrison has written that I haven't read and loved, but her most recent work really moved me. In the novel one of the character says, "What you do to children matters", and it is amazing how that statement is carried throughout the entire book. I loved how Morrison delved into the fact that the way we process our childhoods determines the people we become.

Tell us something about your future writing projects.

As I mentioned above, I have 3 children. 2 daughters (ages 8 and 10), and a son (age 2). For my next writing projects, I would like to write something they can read. My oldest daughter has read some of my poetry, but a lot of what I've written about up until now has been a little too mature for any of them. So, I'm working on a children's picture book, and a book that toes the line between Middle Grade and Young Adult. All of the stories are still speculative fiction, but just a bit more age appropriate for my babies. It's nice being able to run ideas by my kids, read them bits and pieces I'm working on and get their feedback.

You can find Satya on the following social media platforms:
http://satyanelms.com
http://twitter.com/satyanelms

A Song of Vengeance - Andrea Stanet

New York City, 1900

Annabelle

Dozens of enraged red faces bare teeth. In the late afternoon sun clubs, bricks, crowbars, and knives flash in white hands. The mob storms past the theater's front doors like a biblical plague.

The raging men shout: "Kill the niggers!" "Find that coon son of a bitch!" "Them spooks gonna pay!"

I fear we may be trapped here. It won't be long before the crowd busts in seeking the Negro who stabbed an officer during a scuffle a few days ago. The officer had been harassing the man's wife as they routinely do. The paddy must have died, and now we are all in danger.

William, the headliner of our new musical, yanks me by the arm away from the front doors. "We have to get out of here, Annabelle. We'll try to sneak out the cellar and into the alley."

I follow him and a few of the rest of the small cast past the wooden seats, behind the red velvet curtain, and down the rickety steps into the musty underbelly of the theater. Even down here, the air is thick and hot. Underground paths take us back up to the surface. William pushes open the slatted doors, and I climb up into the August daylight.

Almost immediately, we are discovered.

At the mouth of the alley, an officer leans against the brick corner of the building with his arms crossed. He grins. Four men race toward William. Cold sweat trickles down my sides.

The men roar at us. "Where is he? You hidin' that spook in there?"

Without waiting for denials, they grab William. His back arches as a rod smacks into it. "Run, Annabelle!"

I don't want to leave him, but I lift my long, purple skirt and spin toward the opposite end of the alley after the others.

The clack of my boot heels is soon muffled by thundering footfalls. A blow in the center of my spine hurls me forward. My hat flies from my head and lands upside down on the cobblestones like a defenseless turtle. A swarm of feet crushes its green feathers.

The world becomes a blur of white fists and black boots.

Behind it all, soprano screams accompany the dissonance. They come from me.

I try to cover my tender parts. My face crumples inward with a crash, shifting my nose to one side. A tooth slips down my throat. Bones crack and crunch louder than the pounding of my heart.

My cries only stop a second before the scene blinks out to nothing.

#

Josephine

"Papa, you can't do this. It ain't natural, and she wouldn't want it."

"So I should let my youngest daughter die at the hands of those animals?"

My lovely baby sister lay on a table, clinging to the last threads of life. A small group of battered men and women, Negroes helped by some of our white neighbors, brought the bodies of Annabelle and William to the back room of Papa's mortuary. My fiancée was already gone. Before departing, the kind folk who returned them to us warned us not to venture below 50th Street for a few days. The Tenderloin district was pure chaos as a lynch mob punished the Negro community.

But what did that have to do with my Annabelle? Her only "crime" was making beautiful music to bring a little joy and peace to the masses. At 18, she had only just started to live when those white devils silenced her song. What they had done to her delicate body—the thought ripped a hole in my chest.

And my William...

Still, what Papa was suggesting now...

His friend, Mr. Avery, had pale streaks down his pink cheeks forming a pattern to match the tears streaming from Papa's swollen, amber eyes. They each had their shirtsleeves rolled to their elbows and their top buttons undone. Blood stained their fronts.

They retreated behind curtained French doors to continue their whispers, but through a gap, I could see them gesticulating and tearing at their hair. Grieving. Would Papa heed my pleas?

I told them.

For three days and nights, they secluded themselves in the cellar, attempting to reanimate the remnants of my dear Annabelle's body. For three days and nights, I begged them to stop.

Reconsider.

Let her go.

Before this latest reign of terror, they had been determined to create automatons for protection—an invincible, flying army for the Negro community against the violent mobs that plagued the streets every few months. Controlled by sorcery, the mechanized nocturnal predators would bite and slice with the curved blades of their claws.

Annabelle's murder inspired Mr. Avery to add a new dimension to the scheme he and Papa had developed. Reclaim the fallen and turn them into indestructible soldiers.

My sweet Annabelle was no soldier. They simply could not bear to say goodbye.

I implored, "Please, Papa—you can't bind her free spirit to a movable statue. If you need to experiment, take William. Don't do this to Annabelle. She'll never forgive you."

It wasn't that I wanted my fiancée back more than my sister, rather I understood the anguish she'd endure. Likewise, I knew that William, a vocal opponent against the violence perpetrated against our communities, would relish rebirth as an invincible warrior.

But it was not to be. Neither Papa nor Mr. Avery could see their way clear to letting her move on toward peace in the afterlife. Their selfishness ruined us all.

#

Annabelle

I witness the scene from above my mangled remains.

They remove my upper torso and place it into a bronze, avian receptacle, metal chips layered like feathers down its folded wings. From my vantage point over it all, I long to stop this travesty. I am powerless.

After fitting me into my new form, they seal me in with molten bronze, leaving only my face and neck exposed. They hold their hands over me and chant foreign words until black smoke wafts in through the window, into my mouth, eyes, and nose.

My new vessel emits a crimson glow, and the chanting becomes louder. I feel myself being sucked down, down, down. The world goes black again.

I open my eyes to a stark-white, familiar room. Orange filaments glare inside light bulbs. Frigid air against my cheeks reminds me that this room always gave me a chill, yet I only feel the cold on my face. Shifting my eyes side to side, I perceive white shelves holding bottles, vials, and small square file boxes.

Behind me, I know that a white cabinet with glass windows has brown bottles of embalming chemicals. Next to the cabinet, a grandfather clock ticks the seconds by. A diagram of the human body covers the wall before me.

To my left, another table is laden with a sheet-covered body. As I turn my head for a better look, a scraping sound grates on my nerves. What has happened?

I remember the riot, yet I cannot feel the surface of the hard gurney I must be on. Did those monsters paralyze me? And who is the victim beside me? I ache to think that it might be William. I need answers.

"Hello? Papa! Someone! Help me!"

A bustle of movement precedes quick steps, and then the door bursts open with a bang.

"Annabelle, my baby girl. You're all right."

His face, ashen and unshaven, looms over me. Next to him, Mr. Avery's eyes are wide, but his jaw is tight and strained. Josephine's hands partly cover a scowl. This expression my sister rarely wears is worrisome.

"Papa, what's happened to me?" My voice is scratchy to my ears, like when I first wake in the morning. "Last I recall… I can't feel my body. What's wrong with me?"

His dark hands, so dexterous when preserving the bodies of our neighbors who have passed on, clasp my cheeks, but his gaze avoids me. Have I been beaten so badly I've become hideous to my own beloved father?

"Anna…"

When he doesn't continue, Josephine spits words like an angry cat. "Tell her, Papa. Tell her what you and Mr. Avery have done."

Papa traces a line across my forehead and then covers his own face with both hands. He weeps. "It was the only way. You were so… broken."

I can hardly understand the individual words that squeeze between sobs. "Papa?" Confusion forces flashes of the attack to the front of my mind, seeking any clue as to the extent of the damage done to me. I know that I am not anesthetized because my thoughts are clear. If I can no longer walk, my career is over. Will I still be able to sing?

A horrified squeak escapes my lips. "Someone tell me," I cry. "Josie?"

Her expression softens as silent tears cascade down her round, brown face, but she fixes her eyes on me, telling me that no matter what happens, my sister is with me.

Papa finally hiccups and gains enough control to answer me. "The rioters, they left you for dead. By the time your cast mates brought you here, you were barely breathing. We couldn't get through the mob down to the Negro infirmary in Little Africa. The other hospitals wouldn't take you even if we could get to them. You… you died. Right before my eyes." Sobs take over, and he breaks down. I still don't comprehend.

Mr. Avery steps forward, his bowler pressed to his chest, and places a pale, wrinkled hand on Papa's shoulder. He and Papa have been friends for a long time, since I was a little girl. They've been spending more time together than usual, sequestered upstairs in our living quarters or at Mr. Avery's home on the next street. While he has always taken a passing interest in my aspirations, lately he has been more attentive than usual. He's an attractive man, if a tad old. I don't believe Papa knows about the letters he's sent me.

"Annabelle, with the violence against your people happening more frequently, your father and I have been working on a way for you—Negroes—to protect yourselves. To fight back. The police won't help. They're as much a part of the problem as anyone else. When we lost you, I offered your father a way…"

Josephine has always hinted that Mr. Avery fiddled with things—unnatural things. Magical things. Sorcery and beyond. But Papa would never…

"We—your father and I—had designed several… prototypes and had been ready to attempt a ritual to animate them into automatons when all this transpired. Instead, we brought you back, Annabelle. We couldn't repair your body, so we gave you a new one."

Necromancy. In all the rumors about secret societies, all sorcerers, spiritualists, and magi frown upon necromancy. I recall my grandmama's tales of the gods and goddesses of our African ancestors. She also told of Voodoun priests brought to the Caribbean plantations. They would raise zombies and control them. Unlike the legends of the powerful Oya and Chango, those stories of slaves making slaves always angered me with their abnormality and immorality.

Mr. Avery's black mustache twitches against his ivory skin as he waits for my response. No one breathes.

A surge of fury courses through me as images flood my mind. After recalling the horror practiced on me, I now turn my head to glare at Papa and his accomplice. How dare they decide this for me—to die or become their puppet? Death would have been my choice, every time. My motion brings the scratching sound that I realize is my head against the table. From the corner of my eye, I see movement. Gentle rustling accompanies metallic grinding, like small gears moving against each other. An extended wing glints beneath the overhead lights.

Rage blinds me. A long, high shriek that sounds nothing like me escapes my lips.

In stealing the peace of death they have corrupted the one thing that would have made it all bearable—my voice.

#

Josephine

All that remained of my sister was her face, ears, and of course her throat. A half helmet replaced her lovely, thick curls. A three-foot avian container now constrained a larger-than-life spirit.

When they told her what they had done, vexation sparked in her brown eyes. Her wings five feet across, flared. She crashed, shrieking, through the windows and into the night. We rushed to try and stop her. Talon marks scored the windowsill.

Papa shouted after her, attempting to exert his will over her. Mr. Avery chanted a spell and failed as well. Her wrath was too strong.

I felt strangely cold inside and found that I could not muster sympathy for either of the men panicking next to me. "What did you expect?" I forced the words through clenched teeth.

"Josie—"

"No, Papa! It would have pained me to lose her just as much as you, and I've had William taken from me as well. But I warned you not to fool with this type of magic. Now she's lost to us anyway."

He wiped his eyes and seemed to collect himself. He tucked in his shirttails and strode over to the coat stand. After smoothing the gray wool down over his middle and hips, he plucked his black hat from the top of the coat stand and pulled it over his brow. "No, Josie, you'll see. She caught us by surprise is all. We'll find her, and she'll see reason, or we will force her back. We won't lose her."

Mr. Avery had likewise retrieved his coat and hat. "Y-yes, Josephine. All will be well." The quiver in his voice suggested he already knew he was lying to himself and to me.

"It won't. All the lore warns that with the reanimated, there is always a chance they will seek vengeance. After what she suffered... There is no other choice. You must undo this. Please, Papa, Mr. Avery, release her before it's too late."

#

Annabelle

Hours later, I scan the streets from the roof of the Dufresne Theater, the site of my murder. I track a policeman as he carelessly twirls a baton. The street lamp on the corner emits a low buzz. A blue bowler covers the top half of the copper's face while a sandy mustache obscures the lower half.

My lips press together.

The strapping young man, only a few years older than I was, strides along his beat whistling a jaunty jingle. The round buttons of his uniform gleam beneath a full moon. My head turns to follow his progression down the deserted sidewalk. Apparently, the rioters have had their fill of mayhem for this evening.

Anger sizzles through me as my lips part. My intention is to scream, to draw his attention before striking. Part of my mind wants to stop—this is not who I am. Before I can sort out the conflict between my mind and heart, a song bursts forth. A deep, contralto melody floats down toward my prey.

The notes rise and fall, rich yet unfamiliar to my own hearing, until they reach Paddy's ears.

He stops and looks up. Turning on his boot heels, slowly, deliberately, he retraces his steps toward my sorrowful tune. When he reaches the street lamp, his legs buckle, and he drops to his knees. His wide eyes fix on me, and his mouth opens in silent awe.

I continue humming my lullaby as my wings stretch. I glide down from my perch, claws clicking to the sidewalk. Malicious satisfaction creeps into my thoughts as I peer down upon the flushed face staring at me so raptly. He is utterly under my control. So peaceful. Not much more than a boy.

And I was little more than a girl when a piece of filth in a similar blue uniform watched as the breath was kicked and punched out of me.

I immerse myself in the memory and gaze into the paddy's eyes. Golden light connects us. I will the memory into his consciousness.

His body jerks with the pain of each blow dealt to me. He topples to his side, whimpering as he attempts to shield himself from the phantom assault. A grimace twists his mouth, and he writhes on the ground, experiencing my agony. I allow the torment to continue, relishing his pain as my attackers reveled in mine. I smile as a rush of energy twists my thoughts more until I nearly swoon along with the cracker.

Did he egg on the mob? Had he smashed heads or broken black backs with his baton?

"No, please. Make it stop," he begs.

I stop singing and watch him weep. "Like you bluecoats stopped it when it was done to me? You vow to protect the masses, but instead you incite the crowds. You cheer as innocent men, women, and children are hanged and defiled. You pit neighbor against neighbor for your own sick amusement. Well now, laddy boy, no one in the Tenderloin can defend your kind from me."

My head cocks to one side. Anger tugs me forward, claws raking the ground, desperately flexing in need of action. The urge to tear him apart makes this new body shudder, rustling my feathers and bolts as if a breeze kicked up. Yet some part of me hesitates. Just a boy...

A boy who will likely grow up to abuse girls like me, just like all the other rotten cowards in their fancy blue suits, hiding behind their blood stained badges. He'll grow into a man who will let poor white trash dirty themselves while he watches with a smile on his face.

A single hop brings me next to him. I slice across his throat with a hooked, knife-like nail. I rip and slash until all that remains is a lump of shredded flesh. My haunting song fills the night as his blood pools beneath my talons.

#

Josephine

"Mr. Avery," I said as a church bell chimed midnight, "where would a discontented spirit go?" A light breeze tried to snatch my bonnet.

"The most logical place to start would be at the site of her... where the attack took place."

Papa trailed behind us, reluctant to do what he surely understood he and Mr. Avery must do. We trudged down the long blocks south from the upper edge of the Tenderloin down to 44th Street.

With each step closer to the theater, the sounds of voices and activity were amplified. When we turned the corner onto 7th Avenue, from the top of the block, we saw wagons and policemen. Beneath the light post down the street, a white sheet covered a figure. We froze in our tracks.

Without needing to be told, Mr. Avery continued toward the officers while Papa and I eased back into the shadows. A few moments later, he returned, and under the lamplight, he was paler than the moon above.

"Sh-shredded." Mr. Avery gagged, pressed his fingers over his mouth, and then continued in a strangled whisper. "One of theirs. A policeman. It had to be her, but how could she—" Unable to finish, he sobbed into his hands.

I knew exactly how she could do such a thing—it wasn't our Annabelle. It was merely what was left after the best parts of her were stolen from this world. I prayed we could find her before she struck again and further damaged her remaining soul.

Backtracking, we entered the theater through a back entrance and checked the attic. The small, round window, inviting the moonlight in, was dusty and undisturbed. We crept up through a trap door and onto the roof. A scan of the surrounding rooftops revealed no sign of the automaton. Annabelle was either gone or well hidden.

The officers below fanned out to search for the vicious murderer of their brother. Little did they know what they would soon face.

Was she out there hunting them as well? I had a dreadful hunch that she might be.

#

Annabelle

My senses are sharper than they have ever been. From high in the air, I see and hear every intricate detail of the streets below. Before the body is discovered and the drunken swine are called back to duty, I hunt.

The first is a dockworker, smelling of hard labor and fish. Is he going home to a wife? Children? I softly sing him to me and lull him into a stupor. I slit his throat quickly before dragging his body, creating the trail I want the coppers to follow into the heart of the Tenderloin. The thrill makes me quake with anticipation for my next exploit.

The second is a beat cop. His feet drag, and his shoulders slump down. My song to him is harsher. I force the memories into his mind before I plunge my claws into his chest and tear out his heart. He is not the one I seek.

I soar above the rooftops, hunting, searching. In the shadows of an alley, I witness a streetwalker taking money from yet another cop. He spins her forcefully and lifts the back of her filthy dress. Across the street from them, I spy a rope dangling from a streetlight. Anger bubbles up within me.

His animalistic grunts, as if he is nothing more than a rutting dog, assault my ears. And they treat us like animals. Did he take part in lynching whoever hung from that nearby rope? My teeth gnash.

When I was Annabelle, I had no knowledge of a man. Is this to be my first experience with the act of physical love? The only one? The girl who was Annabelle will never experience it or even the raw passion of lust firsthand. A growl rumbles out of me.

Stealthily, I swoop down. I see his face clearly and scream my rage into the night.

It is him! The one who watched my brutal murder with a smile on his face.

My hooks grip his throat. I haul him up roughly. With one hard shake, his neck snaps.

Justice!

The prostitute screams and runs down the avenue. Yes, I think, bring them to me.

I drop him like a sack of rotten potatoes at the base of the light pole. And then I pause. His genitals dangle limply out of his trousers.

With a glance at the rope above, I wonder if white men disfigured the rope's last victim the way they've done to other black men. My jaw tightens. My talons clack loudly as I step between my prey's legs. I grip his flaccid member. I wrench it from him and drop the dead flesh onto his lap. After cutting the rope down, I wind it around his neck. Finally, I soar back to the theater to wait.

The building across from the theater has a side door with a deep overhang that offers me shelter and concealment from the filthy crackers examining my work. Now that I know the power of my voice to draw the uniformed scoundrels to me, I wait and observe.

The body is loaded into a wagon, and most of the coppers split off into teams. They are stumbling right into my trap. My mouth salivates, tasting the bloody nightmare I will soon unleash upon them. I will tear them apart one by one.

When the cart begins its noisy roll toward the morgue, I take flight. I must be in position when my enemy arrives.

Soon, my song weaves through a lazy mist rising up through the cobblestones. I enrapture them, calling them to me where I exhaled my last breath. They bow to my magic. One by one they gather, entranced like the Voudoun zombies of grandmama's stories. And I am their master.

As I envision death and murder, I force the truth into their collective mind. My memories consume their thoughts. The images combined with the melody are so powerful that the scene manifests before them—a stage play to disturb and disgust and terrify. My spectral form floats broken and bloodied atop the bed of night fog. Then I reveal the fate of my first victim slice by slice. They look on in horror but are unable to escape the torturous visions.

The older ones remain stoic. Twitchy fingers and pursed lips reveal their inner revulsion. A few of the younger ones vomit up their suppers. Do they envision themselves shredded like the first of them to pay for their collective sins? Will they cry the way he did, filled with fear and guilt and shame?

I spot my next target—strong and young. Why should he reap the benefits of a long life when my own was stolen from me? I could not even find solace in the peace of death, thanks to Papa and Mr. Avery. I suppose I should feel some measure of gratitude toward them. Without this body—these wings—I would never have had the means to avenge myself.

That doesn't excuse what they've done. They've made me a monster. Some small piece of my mind remains Annabelle, and she is horrified. The old Annabelle wanted nothing more than to fill the world with music. There was love in her heart, not the hatred and thirst for blood that resides there now.

#

Josephine

"Papa, Mr. Avery, look." I pointed toward the last of the officers to leave the scene.

A deep, sad tune faintly reached my ears. The policemen must have heard it too. They froze and then, in unison, turned toward the voice and began to shuffle toward it.

I swiveled to see why Papa and Mr. Avery didn't say anything. They also appeared to be in a trance and followed the song.

I knew the source of the music. Even transformed from the high, light pitch it once was, I knew my sister's voice as well as my own. She was summoning them to her like a mama duck corralling her young… if that mama duck intended to devour the ducklings. I had to save her from her own ferocity for everyone's sake.

As we followed the path of death that she left behind, I knew that if we failed, the Tenderloin, maybe all of New York, would be doomed.

#

Annabelle

A feeling of power that I've only ever known through song surges through me as more and more men flock to my call. They come from the streets, from the pubs, from their homes. They cannot resist my allure, and this knowledge fills me with a rush of superiority. I am a goddess of legend! I feel the force of Oya's tempests churning inside me. I can lay waste to all before me, if I choose.

This new energy within me is dizzying. Strength infuses me as if I still have intact muscle and tendons instead of gears and springs.

As my song amplifies, Papa and Mr. Avery join the crowd of over one hundred men. They have done this to me. The memories begin to accompany my melody, which takes on more minor keys and deeper notes.

I remember everything. I am not a goddess but a monster, a predator, a dealer of death.

The visions I force the crowd to witness become frenzied, repeating faster, honing in on the most brutal moments. They— all of them—will acknowledge the damage they've done and brought upon themselves.

Papa bawls as the picture of my face being crushed with fists and boots repeats relentlessly. My teeth grind as I struggle to keep the song, my source of power, squeezing out of me.

My eyes meet Mr. Avery's, and fury overwhelms me. "You!" My song stops. The images continue, growing and stretching until they paint the entire night sky for all to see. The spell I've woven diminishes but does not break.

All around me, men drop to the ground, covering their eyes, squeezing the sides of their heads. They moan and blubber pleas and apologies—shame in all its forms.

It's not enough. If anything, it only fuels my fire.

"Stop your sniveling, all of you! You fear me, but this is what you've created with your hatred and wickedness." I begin to shake as my inner storm builds.

I turn to a shabby man. His boots are scuffed with holes worn through the sides and toes. His mended cotton shirt hangs limply over patched woolen trousers. I point the tip of my left wing toward him. "You've done this every time you knocked a Negro down to feel like you've got a higher station in your pathetic life." Red sparks shoot from the tip of my wing. They singe the man's scruffy face.

My head whips to the other side of the crowd where the young copper's shoulders shake from his quiet sobs into his blue cap. My right wing sweeps across the crowd and points at him. A streak of white lightning zips out of me and lands at his feet. He looks up at me. His wet eyes bulge. His teeth are now bared, not threatening but in a grimace.

"And you! You cowards lie and cheat—" Each slow word draws another bolt of lightning from me. "—beat and harass. All for your entertainment. Are you entertained now?" My last words crescendo until my voice booms and echoes through the canyon of brick and mortar. One more bolt hits the cop in the chest. He collapses, dead.

Shocked, I try to breathe, but I have no lungs. The part of me that is Annabelle struggles to regain control. There isn't enough of her left. My gaze falls back on Papa and Mr. Avery.

I hiss at them. "You should have let me die. Instead you've turned me into an abomination!" My wings expand and begin to beat, forward and back. Wind speeds and cyclones, swallowing all the men's shouts. My voice rises above all the din. "Do you expect mercy now?"

Not a goddess.

A demon.

My body rises into the air. I hover over Mr. Avery. "Does your friend know about the letters you've sent to me? About your dirty thoughts? How you've begged for my affections? What will you beg for now?"

I swoop down and clench my talons around his shoulders. Lifting him up, I ascend past windows, past rooftops. Lightning cracks from the sky to the ground below. Still the images of violence glow eerily against the darkness. The captivated throng below is powerless to run or to stop me.

Papa shouts up to me. "Please, Annabelle! We only meant to help you!"

"For what? For your army? Or because you—he—was too selfish to let me go?"

With a shriek, I dive. Mr. Avery's body slams into the stone street. I crush him beneath me. He coughs and tries to crawl away. Using my wings to rise, I pound my feet into his spine over and over until he breaks and ceases to move.

And then, like a whisper on a breeze, a familiar sound reaches my keen hearing through the chaos of the wild tempest. "Annabelle! What have you done?"

Josephine. She should not be here.

#

Josephine

She killed him.

Not in a cold-blooded way that suggested she was beyond redemption. But... she killed him.

Her scowl silently roared against generations of pain and oppression. The hunch of her neck echoed the strain and suffering of every lynching victim for countless yesterdays. The flame in her eyes was that of a trapped animal that refused to give in without a battle.

Where had my beloved sister gone? I didn't want to feel sorry for these men, including Mr. Avery. Yet I couldn't allow her to punish them—innocent and guilty alike—for the circumstances of their birth any more than I could condone their oppression of my people for ours. I had to help Annabelle, but how? She had just murdered the only person who could release her spirit.

Or had she?

I searched my mind for all the stories and legends Grandmama had told us as children. As Annabelle moved toward Papa, the answer came to me. "Anna, don't!"

She stepped toward me, hatred and fear warring against her true, peaceful nature and against her love for me. Our eyes locked. As if a glass bubble formed around us, the chaos and turmoil around us faded into the background.

"Please, you have to stop. It's not too late."

"Leave, Josephine," she snarled. "They must pay. If you try to deny me justice..."

"Justice or vengeance? You can stop. Free yourself. Find peace. Isn't that what you really want? The peace that was denied to you?"

The air around her crackled. She glared at me and stepped closer. "I'm warning you...Josephine?" When she spoke my name, for the briefest moment, her voice lost the gravelly reverberation it had taken on.

I heard the clear, sweet tones of my baby sister. She wasn't lost to me yet.

I grasped at the opportunity. "Sing to me, Annabelle. Sing me a lullaby. Do you remember the one?"

Confusion wrenched her features, and her head tilted to one side.

"The one Grandmama used to sing to us."

If anything could break the spell binding Annabelle's restless spirit to that infernal machine, it would be music. Not the discordant, sad song that had drawn these men to her, but a melody of our ancestors—a chant sung to us by our grandmother, who was taught it by her grandmother before her, who brought it with her from her homeland across the sea.

I prayed the song would connect Annabelle to the women of our bloodline who had suffered, as she had, at the hands of misguided or plain evil men.

She began to sing. "Yemaya assessu, assessu Yamaya…" Her voice scratched and choked at first. As she remembered the words, it smoothed and lifted into the crystalline tone so familiar to my heart. The crowd of men surrounding her stilled as her music—the real Annabelle's music—wove a different spell among them.

They cried still, but their tears cleansed rather than tormented. Perhaps some good would come of Papa's and Mr. Avery's actions after all.

Annabelle repeated the soothing melody. Her vocals strengthened with each refrain. Soon, a pale blue light formed a halo around her where she stood, her wings outstretched, her face lifted to the bright moon. The sky's horrific images coalesced and transformed into a majestic, dark woman in blue, adorned with a shell crown and necklace—Yemaya, the ocean mother.

Her hands enveloped Annabelle. Their light intensified. Their glow became a blinding blue sun with Annabelle at its core.

When the music stopped, the brilliance gave one final pulse. The men shielded their eyes. Not me. Tears flowing, I bore witness to the end.

When the afterglow dimmed, all that remained was a bronze shell filled with ash. Annabelle was gone.

Slowly, the crowd dispersed, and most of the confused men went back to their business. Mr. Avery and the slain policeman were carried to the nearest station by some of the bystanders. Papa knelt next to the charred automaton as if something in him had broken along with it.

I could have gone to him. Possibly, I should have. Instead, I turned around and began the lonely walk home.

# # #

Annabelle

Days after my spirit finds its release from its bronze prison, I float high above Josephine as she boards a train bound for Canada. Papa tried to convince her to stay, but she says she can't forgive him. I believe she will. In time.

Now that I am free, I will watch over and guide her until the day comes when we can be together again. In the meantime, I will surround her with the healing of my songs.

Interview with Andrea Stanet

What was your inspiration for this story?

While doing research for a couple of open submission calls, I came across the story of a race riot that took place in the summer of 1900. The events fascinated and stuck with me, particularly in light of the systemic violence that has been illuminated so much these past few years and the Black Lives Matter movement. The time period lent itself well to a steam punk flavor, which I've always been interested in trying. It all flowed together from there.

Why did you choose a black woman for your main character?

As a black woman, it's who I naturally identify with most. Also, at the time of the riot, a black woman was central to the events that unfolded. She was being harassed by a cop, and her significant other intervened. So, it made sense to have a black, female character at the forefront of the story, which eventually turned into two black females.

I spent a good deal of time thinking about the repression of black women then and now, about how we come together to support each other, and about responses to a patriarchy that attempts to stifle women as a whole. Annabelle and Josephine, sisters, represent two possible reactions to this type of oppression.

Why did you want to submit to Black Girl Magic Lit Magazine?

There's been a lot of talk lately about diversity in literature, which is a wonderful thing. Yet, it's still challenging to find a home for a story with themes or characters that don't necessarily fit the mainstream. One problem is that "diversity" is often still expected to represent stereotypes, so if an author strays from that, the work can be seen as less than authentic. (Which is amusing because I think authors are pretty well versed in their own realities and what's authentic within those realities. But whatever.) I feel that Black Girl Magic Lit Magazine has a vision that embraces different voices without trying to impose those artificial and stereotypical expectations. On the contrary, this magazine seems to want to break those molds and open the field for a much wider array of styles and experiences than the typical gatekeepers allow.

I think Black Girl Magic Lit Magazine will fill a much needed niche. We need a showcase for genre fiction that doesn't necessarily express the white, male perspective that currently dominates the playing field. I have nothing against them and am a fan of many of those voices, but as a reader it will be nice to have more to choose from.

What are your favorite novels or short stories and why?

There are way too many to name! I feel like I should start listing some serious and literary titles, but in the interest of keeping it real, I will admit that for better or worse, I always have been and always will be a Stephen King fan. My favorite novels of his are *It* and *The Gunslinger*. I also love the Harry Potter series. My go-to genres are fantasy and horror in general, but my reading tastes can be eclectic. I enjoy Japanese manga and The Flash comics just as much as James Baldwin--it all depends on what I'm in the mood for at any given time.

Tell us something about your future writing projects.

I'm currently working on a fantasy novel about a shapeshifting mercenary who works with fey (fairy) king to combat vampires. I'm also in the drafting phase of a YA contemporary novel about a young girl trying to save her brother from self-destruction by finishing a marathon. I have a couple of other short stories in progress as well--one is a horror about a lake, the other is another YA contemporary that I can't say more about without giving away too much.

You can find Andrea on the following social media platforms:
http://andreastanet.com
https://www.facebook.com/AndreaStanetauthor

Mutts of Kalunga - Jennifer L. Meacham

My story, like so many others, began in death.

Earth was dying; the communities had been consumed by squalor. The water was no longer safe, and food was scarcer than a secure corner to lay your head at night. Thirty-five years ago, mankind began to infiltrate the earth-like planets found within the Kingdom Galaxy. Of the scores of planets revolving around their massive star, dozens had not only landmass, but also appropriate air conditions, climate and life-sustaining water. Twenty-Five years ago, mankind struck a deal with the life forms found in our new home. We had been allowed to colonize their planet under the promise that we would not bring war which had enveloped so many other planets. My parents had been amid the frontiers brought here. My father had been a professor, and my mother was what had come to be known as an Alien Anthropologist.

They and their team had been studying the ancient history of a land known as Africa on planet Earth. We were told that Africans had been the earliest people on Earth, and it had been presumed that understanding mankind's earliest cultures could help us in the new worlds. As a result, much of our world, and the inhabitants therein, were named after different aspects of folktales, history, myths, and beliefs held by Africans long ago. However, my generation never knew anything before this world. The terms, names, and mixed language from days long gone belonged only to our present day.

Of course, the agreements that had been struck to allow our immersion into this world had been nothing but lies. We had since come to understand the true reason these creatures had allowed us to infiltrate their world. We had become their slaves, their newest food supply. Our parents, our founding-leaders, had thought them to be undeveloped, believed our kind superior to them, but they'd been wrong. As humans moved into other parts of the new galaxy, joining less harsh environments, the troubles we faced became tedious to the outlying humans. The inhabitants of kinder worlds which had easily been conquered believed it too much trouble to render aid to our own sad little planet.

And so, mankind had broken all ties with us, the orphans of a lost cause. With no allies we quickly came to terms with what we must do to survive.

We had become warriors. Those of us who were able fought to save who we could and in honor of those we couldn't. My thoughts kept returning to my lessons, to what we had been told, and what we were destined to become as my mind tiptoed into awareness. Suddenly, like a wave washing over me, I recalled being attacked from behind, but by who? By what?

Rain. Freezing raindrops fell to my face where I lay. Where was I?

The chain rattled ominously as I shifted to sit in an upright position in the muck. Icy cold rain fell from the roiling skies, easily finding me between the iron bars above my head. All four walls of my enclosure appeared to be made of corrugated steel, rusted by years of neglect. Water rolled down my face, shivering down my body as my thick black curls clung to my forehead and neck. My tattered clothing clung to my dark skin as I rubbed at my raw ankle. I was barely able to snake two fingers between the rough metal cuff which bound me to the walls. From where I sat within the metal cube of no more than four feet, I couldn't determine direction. Night had taken hold, having snuffed out the light from the sun. At this time of year, darkness ruled our world here on Kalunga for twenty-two of our thirty hour days.

Thunder cracked angrily even as the bolt of lightning still shattered the sky. As if the display had opened a floodgate, the rain grew stronger, more frigid. I moved my hands along the wall closest to me, driving my frozen fingers deeper into the bog that served as our ground. Regardless of how far I dug, the steel walls continued. I felt along the perimeter of my cage and found no weakness to exploit.

Though I knew my weapons and radio had surely been confiscated upon my capture, I did a quick check for same. Finding none, I plopped back down into the fetid mud, sinking as much of myself into it as possible. There could be no escaping the frigid water, but if I could at least avoid the freezing air, I might be able to stave off hypothermia long enough... long enough for an opportunity to present itself.

I had been held in a hive before and had escaped within days. I needed only survive long enough to do so again. As a Suk Warrior, I had trained all my life. They couldn't keep me here. I wasn't their pawn, and I sure as hell didn't belong to them.

My name was Oya Mossi, and I belonged to no one.

As I stopped moving and listened to the torrent of raindrops along the metal construction of the hive I could hear the despair growing. Each cry for help, anguished plea, and moan of helplessness inspired more voices to call out. Soon, the sound of misery competed with the fury of the storm. Men, women, children... they all cried out into the night if for nothing more than to voice their misery. I made no sound as my breath continued to crystallize in front of me but instead, I listened to the waves their emotion spread into the night. Voices grew hushed in small pockets, in pockets that moved about the enclosures. As the quiet neared, the storm too began to whisper. In its place came the familiar grunts and snarls I had expected. As the stillness grew nearer still, I could hear the haphazard click, click of their claws along the iron bars they walked upon.

Another flash of lightening and crack of thunder called up startled voices from the hive. I remained silent as every numb muscle in my body grew taught. The putrid stench of blood, death, and time-worn misery encircled me.

A mutt was near.

The smell of those they'd killed, those they'd toyed with and consumed clung to their tufts of mottled black fur, as did the rot and decay, the filth and excrement they lived amid. The smell was nausea-inducing in ordinary circumstances. But in that moment, the stink of the nearing biloko mutt brought opportunity.

I could hear the biloko licking its chops, continuing to grumble no more than two cages over, even as the melodious bells at its collar jingled sweetly.

Click. Click.

The claws picked over the next cage. Only one more to go.

Click. Click.

A sodden black paw the size of a pumpkin landed on the bars above my head, its five inch claws protruding into my cage between the bars like talons around a branch. Another paw.

Click. Click.

As the biloko was passing onto the next pod I lunged, grabbing hold of one of its rear talons with all my might, slamming it into the iron bar before it with all the force I could summon from within my muddy hell.

The biloko let out a guttural roar, highlighted by an ear ringing screech of outrage. I kept my face upturned, close to the bars, my eyes locked on his four brilliantly white eyes and bared my teeth to him in turn as he pounced, digging between the bars. As I had known they would be, his paws were too broad to reach me. Instead, he brought his monstrous face to the bars, howling and screeching even as he bellowed his anger. His pain.

As with all biloko, his lower jaw jutted out, the two lower canines nearly four inches long. The massive jaw opened and closed, revealing and concealing his smaller but still deadly teeth as he continued to sputter. Realizing his paws could not reach me, his black tongue slid out, seeking. I moved from its reach, but never averted my eyes.

"You can't keep me, Mutt." I growled, my voice low and rough from hours without use in the dank dark.

He retracted his tongue back into his mouth and screeched horrendously. He rammed his face into the bars, sneering and snapping at me ferociously.

I brought my own face, teeth still bared, to within a breath of that monstrosity as I dodged his rotten tongue.

Two loud bellows issued hundreds of meters away, braying into the night.

My biloko's head snapped in the direction the call came from. He gave one guttural bray in response and turned back to me, snarling. His breath continued to puff into the air even as the rain began to fall harder. He snapped his massive jaw once more at me before turning to resume his patrol.

Click. Click.

The sneer that had been splayed across my face shifted into a toothy grin that I shared only with the dark and rain in my metal cage. Victoriously, I sank back down into the muck and toyed with my trophy.

In my hand was the talon I had ripped off the biloko mutt. I tapped it victoriously on my propped denim knee. Though it was soundless against the din of the rain, the sound of opportunity and possibility resonated within me.

Click. Click.

Interview with Jennifer L. Meacham

What was your inspiration for this story?
I saw this magazine mentioned on Twitter and was beyond excited to see people actively working to showcase underrepresented voices, especially in the Sci-Fi world. I knew I had to be a part of it. I didn't know where to start and walked outside in the freezing rain, which in Vegas is very rare, and wondered where to begin. I'm not African-American and can't imagine what it must be like to pick up book after book about people that don't look like me, that I can't identify with. I mean, if you do read something featuring an African-American protagonist, it seems to be about slavery. How odd must that be? For someone, for anything to claim a human being...it's absurd. That person would be a monster and the world that would allow such an atrocity could be nothing but harsh. Thus, Kalunga and its creatures were born.

Why did you choose a black woman for your main character?
I believe that when you create a world, a story, a character, they introduce themselves to you. Yes, I set out to tell a story from a black perspective in this story, but at the end of the day, if she didn't feel genuine, I would have started from scratch. I have another project, (CLOVER America), where that character too is unabashedly strong, amazing and wickedly smart. When I see her in my mind, she's black. I can't explain it. My characters are their own people, and as I shape and mold them, I get to know them. When I meet them, they are who they are, and I don't change their race, their beliefs, or any other aspect about them. Oya Mossi is no exception.

Why did you want to submit to Black Girl Magic Lit Magazine?

It's like I said earlier, I ardently believe we need more diversity in our books, our literature, in every aspect of modern life. The creative worlds are supposed to reflect the real world, and right now, we're not even close to attaining that vision. I do think we've taken massive steps in the right direction over the past few generations, but we are simply not there yet. However, this magazine is another step down the right path and I am so happy to be a part of it!

What are your favorite novels or short stories and why?

Oh boy, it would take a thousand pages to truly answer this. Wuthering Heights is definitely toward the top of the list because of the honesty. True love can be painful and difficult, the exact opposite of so many others we read. *Water for Elephants* is another because their male protagonist endured nothing but turmoil, and it was in that storm that he discovered his happiness. *Like a Sister* by Daugharty is another fav, showing that despite being thrown into a personal hell, people really do come out of it. I guess my common theme in my top picks is this: honesty and a tether to real life, not a fairytale.

Tell us something about your future writing projects.
I am working on a series I'd like to get published and am promoting through my blog, CLOVERAmerica.net and have a YA series I am beginning to send out to prospective agents. I've been invited to do a serial fiction series through a subscription based publisher that I am beginning to work on and have even been toying with future chapters of the Kalunga story. It's a wonderful story, and Ms. Mossi is certainly not one to rest in the hive.

You can find Jennifer on the following social media platforms:
http://CLOVERAmerica.net
@MeachamOddshack

Origin Story - Dawn Vogel

Seattle is a city of runners. Every other car has a "13.1" or a "26.2" sticker plastered to it. So when the much-anticipated zombie apocalypse arrived, I longed to be back in the sedentary Midwest.

I'm not a runner. Or rather, I wasn't a runner before. But apparently it was a long hidden talent that came out when I needed it.

Also previously unknown to me, I'm a good climber. Which is how, a week after the zombie apocalypse began, I wound up covered in pine resin, fifty feet up in a tree, with a crowd of the aforementioned zombies waiting for me to fall. I hadn't thought it through before I went up.

By the end of the first twenty hours in a tree, things were looking better and better for the zombies. I managed to wedge myself in between the trunk and a thick branch, but every time I started to drift off, I jerked back awake with that falling sensation you sometimes get when you're starting to sleep. Trust me, it's much worse when you might actually be falling.

I resisted the urge to look at my cell phone to see just how long I'd not managed to sleep this time. The signal was long dead, but I hadn't killed the battery yet. The sun was coming up, but there was a different light coming from the west, behind me, illuminating the zombies who'd hoped they'd be having some tasty breakfast soon. Then I heard the engine--running a little ragged, but it sounded like a big diesel.

From where I was wedged, I couldn't see the truck. But some of the zombies had started running that direction. I pulled myself into a better position by the time the truck hit the stragglers who were still under the tree. No wonder the engine sounded like shit--most of the grill was gone, and there were bits of zombies, still twitching, in the space where it should have been.

Whoever was driving had pulled the semi almost right underneath the tree. I took that as a sign they'd seen me, and I jumped.

It was a good thing they'd stopped before I hit the top of the trailer, or I probably would have rolled right off. But a moment later, the driver jammed on the gas, and I had to hang on to the edge for dear life to stay up top.

Belly crawling across the top of a moving semi is not advisable for the faint of heart, especially when the driver is trying to throw you. I wanted to get up to the cab, to wave to whoever my rescuer was. I suspected they hadn't actually wanted to rescue me when they slammed on the brakes.

I looked back. At least they'd left the zombies in the dust. But the two burly truckers scrambling up to the top of the cab with shotguns didn't look promising.

"Hey, guys", I said. My voice came out as a croak, not all that distant from the sounds the zombies had been making. Shit. I rose to my feet and raised my hands, both of which happened way faster than they should have.

The younger of the two guys leveled his gun at me. In an instant, I dropped flat on my belly. I kept my hands up and tried to make eye contact with either of the truckers. Both of them looked terrified.

The older one fired. I rolled to the right. Then the younger one fired, and I rolled back to the left. I finally found my voice. "Jesus, stop! I'm not a zombie! I'm alive!"

"Nobody alive moves that fast," the older one said, still sighting along the top of his shotgun. But he didn't shoot.

"Yeah, but nobody dead talks that good," the younger one said. His drawl was all but indecipherable for anyone who'd never been to the South. I'd bet good money he'd grown up in Alabama. And from where I was laying, that wasn't good odds for me getting out of this easily.

I took a deep breath, keeping my hands in view. "That's because I'm alive. I haven't been bitten. I'm clean."

The older one raised his gun a few inches. "You willing to prove that?"

Not the answer I expected. "You gonna let me stand up so I can?"

"Naw, not here," he replied. "You got a name?"

"Satchel."

His gun lowered an inch while he stared at me. It wasn't aimed straight at me, but I didn't like the look of regardless. I considered whether I'd have better odds dodging another slug or trying my luck with the zombies below. When he finally spoke, he asked, "Like the baseball player?"

"That's right. My dad was a big fan. I grew up hearing all about him."

"Well then. I'm Keene, this is Pete." He looked pointedly at Pete, who lowered his gun too. "If you don't mind, we're gonna take a little drive. Gonna have to ask you to ride up top."

I couldn't believe being named after a baseball player was going to be the thing that kept these rednecks from killing me. "Mind telling me where we're off to?"

Keene had the decency to blush. "We ain't gonna ask you to prove you haven't been bitten and are just hiding it under your clothes. There's a doctor holed up not too far from here, a woman. Thought we'd ask her to check you over."

I forced a smile. "That's decent of you. Won't bother you if I find some place back here to hang on a little better?"

Pete turned toward Keene, acting like I wasn't even there. "If she's still got a pulse--"

"You gonna check for it?" Keene asked him.

Pete watched me as he put his gun on the roof of the trailer. "We good?" His voice trembled.

I stretched my right arm as far out in front of me as I could. I turned my head to the side. "Promise I won't bite."

A moment later, warm fingers brushed across my wrist. They stayed there longer than I thought they'd need to, with the way my heart was still racing. "Yeah, okay, she's good," Pete said.

"Alright, let's go," Keene said, turning back to the cab.

I picked myself up from the roof of the trailer and muttered, "Much obliged".

###

The residential streets of Seattle weren't meant for semis to drive on. And since about half of the inhabitants of this particular neighborhood had decided parking rules went out the window when the first zombies rose, the ride was a lot more harrowing than I'd have preferred. At least the few car alarms still going off had dulled to faint bleats.

Keene stopped the semi in front of a high rise apartment building, but kept the engine running. The place was swarming with zombies. I looked at him. "How do we get through the horde?"

Pete sighed. "We use the door to bash any zombies that get near us and get up on the trailer. Then Keene drives under that there fire escape, and up we go. It sucks."

"It sucks worse if I don't find a clear enough spot to stop," Keene replied. "Keep your eyes open."

We circled the building twice, but the zombies were getting even thicker. I looked at Pete. "I'm game if you are."

"You ain't afraid of getting splattered, are you?"

I hesitated. "Define splattered."

"Guts--their guts--on ya?"

"So long as it's not my guts too."

Pete nodded. "Switch me seats. You kick out the door, I'll start shooting."

I looked at him. "Kick, climb, avoid gunshots. And zombies. Great". I hopped on his lap for long enough for each of us to move to the other's seat. Then it was go time.

I grabbed the "oh shit" handle with one hand and the door latch with the other. Just as soon as the door swung open, I was climbing. One hand atop the door, legs trailing up after, and I was on top of the truck, quick as a blink. It was like we weren't even moving. Couldn't say I blamed Keene and Pete for being leery of me.

All the same, if the place hadn't been crawling with zombies, I might have just run. But I didn't. I straddled the light bar on top of the cab and extended one hand down to Pete.

Something clammy brushed up against my hand, and I jerked it back with a yelp. Zombies pressed up against the now mostly closed truck door. Keene was gunning it, but the zombies had converged on us, and when one fell away, the next one in the swarm was right there.

I glanced over my shoulder. The zombies were clustered on the passenger side of the truck, so I spun around and leaned down to tap on Keene's window. He looked like he'd seen a ghost when I crawled farther down to look inside the cab. I mimed rolling down a window, and he obliged, though only a crack.

"Where's the doc?" I asked.

"Hang on." He turned to Pete and said something I couldn't hear. Then he looked at me again. "Get on the trailer, far back as you can."

"There's nothing to hang on to back there."

"Well, you ain't gonna want to be on the cab here in a minute."

I hauled myself back up and did as he said, grumbling under my breath as I went. Again I thought about taking off, but I wasn't counting on my superhuman speed getting me through that many zombies at once. There was just enough of a lip at the back edge of the trailer that I had something to hold on to.

Then I saw what Keene had in mind. On the side of the building, there was a parking garage entrance--wide enough for one car, and with a clear height limitation of 10 feet. He was going to wedge the truck in. Which seemed like a great plan, unless the garage was full of zombies too. Oh, and unless you were outside of the cab.

I searched the wall above the garage. It was nowhere near the fire escape. I'd seen martial arts movies where the masters run straight up walls. I'd climbed a tree. And I was fast now. But was I that fast?

"Only one way to find out, Satch," I murmured.

I had to time it just right. The semi was going to stop in a hurry when the top of the cab hit the entrance.

When it did, time slowed down. I took three steps on the roof and then launched myself at the wall, scrambling as soon as I felt corrugated metal under my fingertips. The toes of my worn out Converse fit right into the grooves in the wall, and I moved.

Only problem was I had no idea where I was going. I stopped once I got to the roof. And scared the living shit out of half a dozen people having a goddamn garden party.

My hands flew up. "Not a zombie!" I shouted. Fortunately, no one on the rooftop was as trigger happy as my buddies downstairs. Or maybe they just weren't armed, like me. Though I did spot one of them gripping a wine bottle like she was ready to break it if she had to. "I'm here to see a doctor."

An older woman, her tight curls gray at the temples, stood up. Not the one who'd grabbed the wine bottle. "That'd be me. Doctor Hayes." Her eyes narrowed. "Who sent you?"

"Keene and Pete. That big crash? That was them." I sighed. "Don't suppose you know if the garage is safe?"

"It should be. The gate is still down. But the power's out, so the gate won't be going up any time soon."

"Can we get down to them, at least, let them know I made it to you?"

Doctor Hayes nodded and started walking. "But I'm going to need some explanation from you as we go. It's not every day a normal young woman scales the side of a twenty story building."

"Yeah, about that." I pointed at myself. "Apparently not normal. Name's Satchel, and I haven't been bitten, but I move like the zombies do."

Doctor Hayes hesitated and glanced back up at the rooftop door we had just passed through. "Does that mean they can scale the wall too?" If she'd been wearing pearls, I think she would have clutched them.

I shrugged. "Look, just because I move like them doesn't mean I know the first thing about them. Aside from the fact that they're dead and eating brains."

"I can't say I know much about them either. But you're not the first person I've heard of who seems to be ... different since the zombies started rising. Betty and R. J. have an old crank powered radio, and R. J. rigged it to transmit as well as receive. We spoke with someone in Tacoma last night who's run across a few ... exceptional individuals."

I arched my eyebrow. "Exceptional?"

"One who can sense zombies in his vicinity, even if he can't see them. Another who seems to be immune to their bite. I've been trying to work up the nerve to get Keene to drive me down to Tacoma, but I suppose he's decided to end his trucker days."

I chuckled for the first time since all of this had started. It felt good. "Any other exceptional folks in Seattle?"

"You're the first I've met," Doctor Hayes said.

I relished the thought of being the only person in Seattle who'd benefited from the zombie apocalypse. But then the little voice in my head that always sounds like my grandmother reminded me not to be selfish.

While I was considering this, Doctor Hayes opened a door on the fifth floor and led me into a bright hallway. "These modern buildings. You can't get all the way to any extreme without changing staircases."

"Any thoughts on how to keep people from mistaking me from a zombie?"

"Well, I imagine you could force yourself to move more slowly, if need be. Though I can't help but think that would be a terrible waste of a miraculous gift."

Now she sounded like my grandmother, and that tipped me firmly into the mindset that I had to use this ability to help people. A sign across the street for a sporting goods store caught my eye. "How many people do you figure are still living out there?"

"There's no way to be sure," she said. "I imagine we'll cluster together in time, rebuild civilization, and all that. At least that's what the movies tell me we're meant to do."

I nodded and walked over to the window. The streets were lined with trees, at least the ones Keene hadn't hit in his madcap drive around the block. It'd be a hell of a leap to make my way from one side to the other just in the trees, but it looked like it could be done. The doors to the shop had already been smashed in.

"Well, it's going to take a catalyst. Most things do. Tell you what. You check me out, make sure I'm not harboring some weird strain of whatever is turning everyone into zombies. But then, I've got some catalyzing to do."

"What do you mean?"

I grinned. "I bet I can outrun these zombies. And I know a couple stretches of I-5 where I can practice." I gestured at the store. "You gotta figure no one's going to miss their stock of size 8s, right?"

And that's the story of how I became the Seattle Courier.

# # #

Author Interview with Dawn Vogel

What was your inspiration for this story?

A lot of my stories come out of an image or a snippet of dialogue, some of which has its origin in reality. There really are a lot of cars in Seattle that have 13.1 or 26.2 stickers on the back, indicating their drivers have completed a half or whole marathon. I think I was driving behind one of them when I had the idea for a zombie apocalypse in Seattle in which a non-runner (like myself) was trying to survive. The beginning of the story stuck in my head until I wrote it down, and then everything else grew out of that.

Why did you choose a black woman for your main character?

When I first started writing Satchel, I wasn't entirely sure who she was going to be (she didn't have a name at the beginning, either). As the story grew, and her voice became clearer in my head, I figured out who she was, and that was a black woman who had grown up hearing stories of the great black baseball players, including the one she was named after.

Why did you want to submit to Black Girl Magic Lit Magazine?

I love reading and writing stories about diverse characters, and I wanted to contribute to this awesome new endeavor!

What are your favorite novels or short stories and why?

I love pretty much every novel Neil Gaiman has ever written, though I can't choose just one favorite. I read a lot of short fiction, both as an editor and as a reader, but a couple that have stuck with me are "Deacon Carter's Last Dime" by Nathan Crowder and "When I Grow Up" by K. Kitts.

Tell us something about your future writing projects.

At the moment, I'm focusing on short fiction, and I've got a nice mix of fantasy and sci-fi planned in the coming year. I don't often write sci-fi, so that's a nice way to stretch my writing muscles. My topics are all over the place, but lots of alternate history is in the plans.

You can find Dawn on the following social media platforms:
http://historythatneverwas.com
http://twitter.com/historyneverwas
http://www.facebook.com/History-That-Never-Was-Dawn-Vogel-185337324841687/

Issue 2

This issue is dedicated to Lt. Abbie Mills

2013 - 2016

Letter from the Editor

Thank you for joining us on another magical ride for the second issue of *Black Girl Magic Lit Mag*.

So I was scrolling down my Facebook timeline and I saw a post about a black version of the movie Matilda and who would be great for the cast. At first glance I was like *oh that would be great.* I loved the movie Matilda growing up and I loved the actors that people were saying should play these parts, but then I stopped and thought about it.

I thought about all of the writers I know that have written or are writing awesome stories featuring Black characters that are original stories. I'd much rather a new Black creator get put on with the story of their own that didn't have a white precursor than to see the "Black version" of stories that we have already seen. In fact in my opinion having a "Black version" of an already established movie, play, or TV show seems to position the original (white) version as the best version of the story and the Black version as the second tier version, just by the fact that in the act of remaking something you're always holding that second version up to the first in comparison. Which lead me to say to myself, we don't need a Black version of XYZ, what we need are our original stories by Black creatives with Black characters front and center.

Trust me they're out there. There are so many writers, artists, and other creators that I've come into contact with that are creating new, original, funny, heartwarming, scary, fantastic content and they just need the proper vehicle for disseminating it and widespread knowledge of it and when we create a black version of an already established story are we not just pushing our original stories to the back because of the inherent popularity of these original stories. Instead of having a black Matilda I would love to see the movie version of the *Jumbies* by Tracey Batiste, Zetta Elliott's time travel series, or the post-apocalyptic *Orleans by* Sherri L. Smith made into movies. These are original stories with Black characters by Black creators.

So in that vein, in this issue we have a new section spotlighting a Black Creator who is creating wonderful content with Black characters in the spotlight. In this issue we have Sophia Chester who is the writer behind the YA Sci-Fi novel *Cosmic Callisto Caprica and the Missing Rings of Saturn.*

Thanks again for purchasing and we hope you enjoy!!!

Kenesha Williams
Editor-in-Chief

In This Issue

The Stars for a Song
'The Stars for a Song' is a flash fiction piece regarding the creation of the moon by a saddened deity.

Doughnuts
This is a horror/vampire story about a cop killing in NYC. The protagonists are Black women.

World of Rain: Adaeze's Ambition

Sisters
A supernatural story about sisters that can't let each other go.

The Souvenir
A psychic battle with historic significance is waged between two individuals with family ties.

From Peter
From Peter is a whimsical snapshot of the fantastic clashing with reality, all from the perspective a half-Jamaican, half-white lesbian.

The Stars for a Song - Angelicque Bautista

I wove stars into the sky once so that the world would sing.

The corner of darkness that fell over my corner, thick with trees growing from sturdy ground and fed by calm waters, to silence the last of the click-clicks and the tik-tik-tiks along the ground. I had stepped out of the water, saddened, by the barren gift night always gave me. So great was this gift that the click-clicks and tik-tik-tiks from the tiny cricket guests waned and the night's silence ruled.

No amount of encouragement from me was enough. The darkness swallowed up the sky and the crickets failed to see me. My skin was made of the very same and powerful matter—rich with darkness that was warm to the touch but allowed me to fall into the night. When it rained, it was as if I was one with it. Light granted it a beautiful sheen, and the crickets would sing to me about its beauty. They sang along the grounds and bid the trees to grow taller, the dirt below stronger, and cleansed the river's waters. I would dance among them, but our time together was always too short. The crickets rested under the daylight's grace, and awakened only as orange and purple announced the night's arrival.

I grew too tired of losing my friends within the night's silence, and too tired of being swallowed up by its darkness. Before the sun's setting, I spread fingers over fiery plumes of orange and velvet shades of purple and dug deep so as to break off a pinch of white. I had light, blooming within my hands, to fill the sky.

This is how I wove stars, and let the world sing.

Darkness came, and the crickets were silenced. Water rushed angrily against the riverbed, the thick trees grew shadows that loomed dangerously over the rocky ground. The sun rose again to end it, but all too soon waned at day's end. I broke off another bit of light. I used it to paint mountains onto the night sky; dotted canopies along them and spread bright water around. It was strong enough to stick and weak enough to only leave a glow. My job was well and truly done once the crickets began to chirp. Their click-clicks and tik-tik-tiks drew shadows away from the trees and batted at the water's petty roars.

That night was the longest I'd ever seen since I walked out from the deepest, darkest depths of the riverbed. My smile shone pearly under the pock-marked sky and my skin glowed under their misaligned rays. Singing assured me that my cricket friends could see me; their happiness filled me with a precious glow. When the darkness began to fade, I reached up to smear a sphere along the sky and let a new light appear over the world.

I wove stars, and let the moon rise after the sun, so that the world would keep singing.

Author Interview - Angelicque Bautista

Hi, Angelicque Bautista

What was your inspiration for this story?
The inspiration came from an older legend among my people where a young woman was once left waiting for her lover by a hillside; the two were from warring tribes and he had died trying to reach her after they had arranged to runaway together. The moon, taking pity on the waiting woman, turned her into a flamboyan.

Stories like this have always piqued my interest. The way nature and the world becomes a part of our stories was what brought me to this one. I started with a river, and then the crickets, and then a woman. I saw the world through her eyes and wrote out her desires.

Why did you choose a Black woman as your main character?
Blackness is a part of me and though I'm what people consider light-skin there is still a strong presence of Afro-Latina in me; I felt the need express it and as I wrote I couldn't imagine anyone else. All I could see was a woman walking out from still freshwaters, shadows dancing around her and calling her back to them, eager to hear the world sing. Then I tried to see the world through her eyes and wrote the piece.

Why did you want to submit to Black Girl Magic Lit Mag?

I'm still starting out as a writer and I'd seen submission calls after submission calls but one for Black Girl Magic Lit called my attention; it brought to think about all the books I read, and all the heroes and heroines within their pages. I could rarely recall a moment where one was black, or even just not Caucasian, and I felt that contributing to a magazine so uniquely tailored to blackness was a way to contribute. This way there would be more than just white to see—not because whiteness needs to be washed away, or dominated, but because its presence is so strong that everything else seems to fall away. Everything that it is not then becomes less present and there we lose perspectives, and visions of the world that are valid and necessary to see.

What are your favorite novels or short stories?
I try to read a bit of everything but a work I continually return to is Brave New World by Aldous Huxley. His complex writing and perspective on a mechanical, processed, and heavily detailed world took my breath away. In fact, I had read it at a time when I felt English literature had nothing to contribute to me; reading the first few pages showed me there was so much more to learn and understand. It took me more than six months to complete and even then a year to work out symbolism and themes. I still go back to it and find things I had missed before.

Tell us something about your future writing endeavors?
Currently I'm working on a series of short stories trying to represent the desperate and confusing feelings that are enveloping Puerto Rico at the moment. I hope to find a way to not only represent the sense of fear and helplessness but hope and strength that my people carry at this time of great uncertainty.

Thanks for your submission. Where can we find you on Social Media?
http://epiesque.tumblr.com

Doughnuts - Loretta H. Campbell

Unfortunately, there is no mistake," she said, closing the file".

Alberta Finch, the city coroner handed the file folder to Chief Detective Beasley Whitfield.

Whitfield looked at the folder. She ignored the myriad phone calls blaring in the squad room. Three of her officers had died horribly and inexplicably. Whitfield wanted to know how and why. So far, she didn't like what she was learning.

Still, Finch was a thorough and serious woman. She rarely if ever made mistakes.

"None? Whitfield asked pleadingly.

Finch stared at her and said nothing.

Whitfield was getting flustered, something *she* seldom did. She looked out at the early morning traffic and silently prayed for answers.

"The killers must have been animals, and humans put bites there to throw us off..."

"What? Finch said obviously annoyed.

"Yeah, it's easy to get human saliva." Whitfield was reaching and both women knew it.

Finch wasn't having it. She was an old soldier kind of coroner. She didn't believe in guess work. She believed in science. The data was conclusive.

She straightened herself up to her full 5 foot height and said,

"There has been no trace of animal hair, dander, or anything else. Listen, I'm a coroner not a fucking zoologist. The teeth marks were clearly human. People bit and sucked every ounce of blood out of three police officers."

She stopped and wiped her sweating forehead with a lacy handkerchief.

"This is an impossibility. Or a clusterfuck. I don't know which." Beasley replied.

"Beas, that's it. I ran these tests myself *three times.*

"If humans did this, where's the blood? The area around the bodies was clean." Beasley's mind had been filled with the pictures of the three dead cops.

Both women stared at the murder board in Whitfield's office. The men had been killed in their own precinct during one of the worst blackouts in the city's history. It had been a sweltering summer night. Nobody heard anything. The backup generators were enough for the lights but not enough for the department surveillance cameras apparently. The pictures were blurry. One minute the men were talking amiably. The next they were dead in their various grotesque poses.

"I don't know, Beas. That's for you guys to find out anyway. Now, I need sleep. I've been up all night with this. I'm fried."

Finch walked out of Beasley's office leaving the sharp click of 3 inch-stiletto heels in her wake.

A small legion of reporters surrounded her in the lobby and began demanding answers to numerous questions at once. "No comment at this time. This is an ongoing investigation." Finch said getting into her car and driving cautiously through the encircling press.

Beasley was afraid to look out of the window for fear the reporters would see her. They had been trying to storm the battlements of her outer office for days. The make-shift precinct was an old Quonset hut that had been used for storage back in the day. It was the best alternative to the crime scene of the real Precinct 107. It was a strong fortress against the press.

She turned back to her murder board. There in vivid color were the bodies of the three cops. The men were in the same proximity from each other, yet each of them had been killed differently.

On a quiet street near the old Sydenham Hospital, Jamie Webster sprang out of a troubled sleep. Nestled between her cat and dog, she sat up and looked around anxiously.

Both of her pets were fully awake and staring at a point in the middle of the bedroom. There were three bodies scattered around the floor. All were glowing and unnaturally pale.

There were two white policemen. She recognized them because they worked with her uncle Glenn.

Then she saw her uncle or what was left of him. He sat slumped over a desk with his head on the floor. She heard her uncle's voice whisper something. She wasn't sure what it was. The image began to fade.

Jamie started to tremble, then shake violently. After a few seconds, she lost consciousness. Because they were used to their mistress, both pets covered her with their bodies and slept.

Hours later, her mother called with tragic news. Jamie's beloved uncle Glenn was dead.

When there was silence on the other end of the line, her mother said, "You knew. Didn't you?"

More silence.

Finally, Jamie croaked out. "I saw him."

"They won't tell us how he died." Her mother sobbed. "All they said was it was in the line of duty."

"His head was cut off," Jamie said dryly.

"Oh God. Please God." Her mother sobbed again dropping the telephone.

Jamie hung up. She got out of bed and went to the kitchen to feed her animals.

The telephone rang again. "Can you see who did it?" Her mother asked.

"No, but Unk said something. I couldn't understand, but I think it was a name." Jamie said putting the telephone on speaker. She mixed cat food with the dog food and both animals ate. For a few minutes, the only sound was teeth crunching food.

"It couldn't be Nanette. Could it? He broke up with her when…"

"Who's Nanette?" Jamie asked. She was watching her pets eat. Something about that soothed her. For the millionth time, she congratulated herself on getting pets. Jamie was sure that they thought they were brothers. She wondered if they thought they were human.

"Never mind, baby." Her mother said. "What Frankie don't know won't hurt her. Besides, Nanette ain't that kind of crazy."

At the precinct, George stepped in front of the murder board.

"Hot chocolate, Chief?" He asked.

"Thanks," she said extending her hand but not turning from the murder board. She sipped. "Wait, this is cold."

"Yes, it was hot a half an hour ago when I brought it in." He said.

Beasley sighed, "Sorry I didn't hear you come in", but George was already walking out of the room munching on a doughnut. She didn't know how long she had been staring at the murder board. She could hear detectives comparing notes in the other office.

The sound of the voices disturbed her because the killer was still at large. The only constant was George. Beasley liked the way he came and went quietly but efficiently. On the other hand, her husband David thought George was seriously repressed.

"He never talks about himself. He doesn't have a personal life, and he never fucks."

"We don't know that", she had answered

"Listen", David had countered. "I'm a man. We talk about sex whether we're straight or gay. This guy don't talk about nothing."

To David, George was a deviant of some kind hiding out in the police department. "Best place to hide is in plain sight," David said often.

Thinking of her husband, she decided to call him to tell him she wouldn't be home again tonight.

"Hey," she said trying to sound perky.

"Hey back," David said evenly. He clearly wasn't interested in sounding perky. "I'm down the street, so I'll be there in a minute."

"Down the street from where?"

"Headquarters. Or whatever y'all are calling this temporary place."

"David, you can't just come here. We're in the middle of a police investigation."

"I am a police officer on temporary leave, offering assistance in a homicide investigation of fellow police officers." He said testily.

"On leave my ass, you're retired *and* on disability. Besides, you retired from Vice. This is ..." She decided to try another tact. "Don't you have bird watching to do?"

"I can do that anywhere. Plus, I'm alive which is more than you can say for the three dead cops whose deaths you're investigating. I'm volunteering my services. You got a problem with that, take it up with my superior."

"You're being ridiculous."

"Just open the door when I knock." With that the connection ended.

Beasley went back to her murder board. Four of the detectives came into the adjoining room. As she was going to join them, there was a knock on her side door, and her husband came in carrying two large Dunkin Donuts coffee boxes.

"I'm going to talk to the guys," she said avoiding her husband's stare.

"You look like a thrown-away brown paper bag," He said. He walked over and gave her a deep, slow kiss.

"Is that a gun in your pocket? Or, are you just happy to see me?" She asked huskily.

"Actually, baby the gun is in the holster on my shoulder. That's a hard on pressing into your tummy." He pulled her tighter and rubbed his erection across her belly.

"I miss you too", Beasley sighed.

"Vacation when this is over. I know." David said clearing his throat. "Now to the troops."

Beasley walked slowly behind her husband. He was immediately surrounded by former colleagues.

"What's up?" Jacobs said shaking David's hand.

"I was in the neighborhood, thought I'd drop by."

"You're shitting us", Reynolds chimed in giving David a bear hug. David visually flinched at the pressure on his wounded shoulder.

"Fuck man, I'm sorry. I..." Reynolds apologized.

"No worries."

Nobody wanted to comment on the near fatal gunshot wound that David was recovering from.

In an attempt to be light hearted, Maisie said,

"If you can't keep a good cop down, what're you doing here?" She pecked David's cheek.

"Folks ignore this man, he is stalking me." Whitfield said trying to keep the levity going.

Her husband wasn't interested in humor. "I'm here to help." He said a sudden serious tone in his voice.

"The papers made us look like fools," Maisie said with an injured look.

"You want to tell me where you were. Sometimes fresh ears hear something." David offered.

"Me and the chief were at the World Trade Center. We'd gotten a tip about a bomb," Reynolds said.

"I told you about that," Beasley added. "It was a stink bomb—no shrapnel just unadulterated funk."

"Thank you for burning those clothes by the way," Jacobs said picking up a notebook and giving it to David.

With a slow deliberate attention to detail, David Whitfield questioned his former colleagues one by one. Except for Beasley and Reynolds, everyone else had been on different floors of the department at the time of the murders. The shouts of the 8 am crew brought them to the killing floor.

Despite the same old questions, none of the detectives showed signs of annoyance. David was a trusted friend who grieved with them.

Suddenly, Maisie, known for being the toughest cop in the department, broke down and ran into the bathroom to cry. Her colleagues looked away as if they hadn't noticed.

While her husband questioned her subordinates, Beasley checked in with the K-9 unit. Saliva like blood is unique to each individual, Finch had told Beasley. Two of the victims had had salvia in their wounds. Every day the dogs accompanied the detectives and volunteers from other precincts. They questioned dozens of blood ritual cultists. Even imprisoned cannibalistic murderers were questioned in their cells. Some of them might have been in contact with copycat acolytes, Whitfield told her team. Police officers were combing files all over the city looking for clues.

The evidence was slim to none. Still, they had to try whatever they could. Once they found it, they would find the killer or killers.

Just standing in front of the murder board was frustrating. Whitfield had to do something.

She put on her coat and headed for the door. Once again, she would view the actual crime scene. She had to find a lead. Her men were killed horribly, and she had to find the killer.

"Where are you going?" David asked as he walked back into her office.

"Over there," she said pointing with her chin.

"Not tonight," he said taking her arm. "Home and sleep."

"They were my men", she countered.

"And they're dead. They'll be dead from now on. Time to rest, so you can find their killers." David pulled her through the door.

She hesitated but had to admit that he was right. Resigned to fatigue, Whitfield followed her husband. Although she was surprised that George was still in the office, she was so tired that she asked him to tell her team goodnight for her. Thank God for George she thought. It's good he doesn't have a life. It means he's always available. She was too sleepy to even feel sorry for him.

That night Beasley nestled against David and dreamed of the dead cops. In the dream, the murder board was above the bed and, she was examining the pictures.

The veins in Warren's neck looked like limp plastic straws. They were a bluish white completely free of any color. Suddenly, Warren's head tried to speak. Beasley attempted to reconnect the veins and arteries.

She woke up to the smell of hot chocolate.

Beasley lay for a second. She thought about how painful it had been to tell the cops' families about the killings. Death was an occupational hazard for cops. Yet, families are always the same. They are shocked and outraged when their loved ones die. The craziest part was keeping the information out of the papers until the families had been told.

The blackout had been the worst possible problem for Jamie Webster. Although she had a closet full of candles, that light wasn't enough. Plus, the amount of candles she used was a fire hazard, according to Ricky the super. Ricky had gone around to the tenants and offered flashlights and candles. When he got to Jamie's apartment, he had yelped.

"What the fuck? You trying to burn the whole building to the ground?" Ricky was excitable, in Jamie's view. However, she had a hard time explaining that burning 100 candles to illuminate an apartment was perfectly acceptable *during a blackout.*

Ricky was a good super. All of the tenants called him "golden hands". He could fix any machine, except his brain. He was as dumb as bad weather. Jamie gave him a generous tip to calm him down and went to bed under a mountain of comforters. Most of the shadows were banished by the candles. The blackout would save on her usually high electric bill. Now, for once, she couldn't leave the lights on all night.

Later, when the vision woke her up, she realized that thousands of candles would have been useless. She learned that there were things much worse than burning buildings.

Whitfield was awakened by a telephone call during the night.

"Chief Detective Whitfield?"

"Yes, who's this?"

"Jamie Webster. Glenn Warren was my uncle?"

"Oh, you got this number from his wife?"

"Yes, ma'am."

"Of course, I'm very sorry for you loss."

There was silence on the other end of the line.

"Would you like to come by my office? We could talk a little. If that's what you want."

"Yeah. That would be good. Could I come by tomorrow?"

"No problem. Any time is fine."

"Thanks. I'll be there."

Jamie hung up. She picked up her cat with effort. "Scylla, you weigh more than twins." The cat purred loudly and snuggled up to its mistress.

Whitfield, now fully awake, stroked her husband's butt.

"Again?" He murmured.

"All you ever think about is sex," she said half joking.

"Oh yeah, right. Come 'ere Sex." He said pulling his wife closer.

However, Whitfield's sense of contentment was temporary. When she got out of bed later that Saturday morning, she turned on the news. The lead story was about the grisly murder in the largest police precinct in Queens. Three cops were killed with no known witnesses, and the police were not communicating with the press about details. Whitfield followed the smell of food into the kitchen and turned off the TV.

The next morning, Jamie walked into Whitfield's office. Both women were shocked by the other's appearance.

After hearing the sweet melodic voice of Jamie on the telephone, Whitfield expected a young, placid-faced buppie. Instead, she saw a tall blue black woman of about 30. Jamie was bald with a tattoo of an angel behind both ears. She wore a long black dress and red sneakers. She smelled like wet dog fur.

When Jamie extended her hand in greeting, Whitfield had a moment's hesitation before she shook it.

Jamie was equally taken aback by Whitfield's appearance. Here was this brown-skinned woman in a sea of white men. She was short, barely Jamie's mother's height, and her mother was 5 feet. Whitfield had a snow white Afro. Her hair was parted on the side with a beret the color of rubies. Her uniform looked brand new. She was wearing make-up and smelled like sex. Jamie hoped her senses were deceiving her because that wasn't a "professional" smell.

Maybe the smell was some new kind of perfume that buppies were wearing. She could tell that Whitfield was reluctant to shake her hand. That didn't bother her. A lot of people didn't want to look at her. Her look was her armor. Not that it helped any.

"Would you like anything, coffee, tea? We have juice if you want that." Whitfield began.

"Coffee would be okay." Jamie said.

Whitfield had to remember that this voice belonged to the woman on the telephone *and* the one standing in front of her.

"George." Whitfield called.

"Ma'am," George said poking his head in the door.

At that moment, Jamie yelped as if burned.

Both George and Whitfield gave her a questioning look.

"Something wrong?" Whitfield said.

"No, I mean, I don't know. I just got this pain in my head."

"Maybe you'd better sit down. I didn't realize you've been standing this whole time. Sorry".

"I'll get some coffee", George said and ducked out quickly. If he thought Jamie looked odd, he didn't show it. The other detectives seemed to have noticed something, however. They were coming over to her side of the department and pretending to be talking to each other. They kept casually looking into her office. Whitfield drew the blinds and sat down.

"What's that smell," Jamie said taking the seat that Whitfield pulled up for her.

"What smell?"

"It's like blood or something."

"I don't smell anything. Are you...?"

"No, my period was over last week." Are you...?" Jamie asked.

"No not any more thank God." Whitfield said with relief.

Jamie shrugged and sat down.

Jamie cleared her throat and began telling Whitfield about her vision. Whitfield listened because she was trained to. She showed a neutral face, but she thought Jamie was completely insane. The outfit, the tattoos, the dog smell. In fact, everything about Jamie seemed crazy in Whitfield's opinion. She was probably a nice girl underneath all that, but nuts. Case closed. Then Whitfield heard the words "head on the floor". That information had not been shared with the press. Only the killer or killers and the police knew these details.

"Oh my God," Whitfield said out loud. She sat up straighter.

Jamie didn't react. She was used to people thinking she was bonkers when she talked about her visions.

"Sometimes, it takes a little longer for me to remember the words people say in my visions. Unk was trying to tell me a word. I can't remember it yet, but I know it was the killer's name", as Whitfield began to take notes.

On the night of the murders, Vinny woke up and scratched his scrotum. The lice were particularly hungry, he noticed. He took a swig of cheap and plentiful wine and stretched.

His 'partment was the dumpster behind Precinct 107. It hadn't been used for its intended purpose since Vinny took up occupancy 5 years previous. He had to pee, so he climbed over the top and went to the port-a-potty. This too had been in existence for about 5 years. Unofficially, Vinny was a homeless man. In reality, he lived in a dumpster behind a police precinct. Everyone knew him. Over the years, the cops had stopped trying to get him into rehab. Food was left for him in a small pantry off the kitchen.

He was fed on the condition that he never went inside the precinct. Ever. Vinny was not a thief and took pride in telling anyone near or far that he wasn't. He did have a horrible odor. In the summer, his smell could produce nausea in a fishmonger.

After using the toilet, Vinny went to get his dinner. All of a sudden, he noticed something. There were no street lights. He had been using the full moon to navigate. He could see a little up the street. This was a quiet street, but nobody was driving a car. Nobody was out walking a dog. Nothing was happening. Where were the lights? It must be the heat, he thought. He had lived through numerous blackouts.

Most important to him, he was hungry. Very hungry. Whatever it was had to wait until he had eaten. Even he had to have food with his wine. He groped his way to the door and went in. To his relief, there was light inside the precinct. Vinny knew the precinct had a generator. The chief insisted that it be tested regularly despite the fact that it was a loud as a subway train sometimes. It would mask any noise Vinny made, but he was perfectly quiet—as usual.

From the pantry, he could see the desk sergeant writing, and Warren and Carter hovering over a box of doughnuts. He salivated and turned to the boxes left for him.

Just then, the door flew open. All three men turned to see who is was. Vinny was curious until he saw the lights flash. He looked again and saw a man pick up Carter and tear into his body with his hands. Vinny stood as rigid as a stone. It happened so fast that Carter didn't have time to make a sound. The man threw him on the floor like a wad of paper.

Jameson drew his pistol. Before he could fire, the man had picked him up by the throat. The man threw Jameson down so hard his head cracked. Vinny could hear the smack.

The man was moving faster than anything Vinny had ever seen, but Warren was trying to jump him. The man caught Warren in mid-flight by the head—and pulled it off. Then he put Warren in a chair like he had been a naughty boy. He set the head next to Warren as if it was a piece of furniture.

Vinny was so scared that he felt faint. Where were the other cops? That damn noisy generator. Maybe the other cops were dead too.

As Vinny was thinking that, the man started to sniff. Vinny knew his odor would make him a target. He eased out of the door. Over the years, he had learned how to move carefully and silently

He slid over into the dumpster just as the man came to the pantry. Vinny prayed with all his might. Vinny looked through the crack in the dumpster, and watched the man sniffing like a wild animal. His prayers were answered...

He heard wind rushing past the dumpster, and saw the man vanish like fading light. He passed out clutching his bottle and praying.

The next morning, Vinny's brain was clearer. He remembered the nightmare. It had to be a nightmare. Then he heard voices. Everyone was talking about killings. He realized it wasn't a nightmare. Worse, he realized he knew the face of the killer.

Whitfield studied the profile she had had worked up on Jamie Webster. The girl's story sounded insane at the beginning. Still, the details that she gave were conclusive. So much so, that Whitfield had the department psychologist examine Jamie. The girl was sane. Whitfield didn't believe in psychic powers per se. Yet, she had seen cases where psychics had been brought in and gotten excellent results.

Despite this, Whitfield sensed that Jamie was hiding something. It wasn't about the case. It was something personal. Whitfield checked into Jamie's background. She had been a good student but prone to fighting. The girl had a spotty work record. Her most recent job was on a psychic hotline. That was not surprising. It paid the bills apparently. Jamie had her own co-op and little credit card debt. No romantic interests apparently.

For the most part, Jamie's biggest problem was her lack of fashion sense. At least that's the way Whitfield saw it. Because of her talk with Jamie, Whitfield had decided to try something unheard of. Some of the team members weren't happy about it, she knew.

George came in and closed the door behind him. He looked shot to pieces. The overtime made them all look their worst, Whitfield realized.

"Chief, about this saliva check. I mean some of us haven't had any dental work for some time."

"We can't be sloppy about this George. It's essential that we get the most recent information."

"But, you're checking *us*." He said emphatically.

"George," Whitfield with equally emphasis. "There was no way anybody could have gotten in here. No glass was broken on the windows. No doors were jimmied. There was *no forced entry*. The cameras are fucked up, but nobody left the building."

"It's messing with morale, chief." George was clearly trying to appeal to her guilt.

Whitfield disliked this new tact even more than the first one.

"We are looking for a killer, a murderer of one of our own. If it is one of our own, it's better that we deal with him. This isn't going to an arrest, trial, or jury, and we all know that."

Before George could respond, Whitfield turned to the murder board on her computer. She continued making notes.

George left with his usual quiet. For some reason, Whitfield felt that quiet was more about anger than acceptance. She couldn't say he had been insolent. Yet, something about his manner seemed defiant. Although she was surprised by his request, she didn't let him see it. Whitfield had a gut feeling that she was on the right track with the dental records. Her gut had never been wrong. She was the leader of a team, and three of them had been killed.

She knew, everyone knew, that is she didn't catch the killer, the team would never trust her again. Nobody said it to her face, but it was an unspoken truth. So, she had to go at finding the killer the best way. It didn't matter if the team liked her methods. She had to get results. She contacted the head of the New York University Dental School. Usually, she would have had George do that, but she felt a little leery of him at that moment. The testing would be done in a special room set up in the temporary precinct.

The days that followed were the new normal at the precinct. Reporters were trying to get interviews with Whitfield or any of the detectives. The public relations department was busy thinking of new ways to say the same thing. "Ongoing investigation. All possible leads being followed."

Despite all that the dentist came and went discreetly. The reporters thought he was another cop. The public relations people said he was bringing the newest technology in forensic equipment.

It was the third week, and Whitfield felt like she was swimming through mud. That feeling got worse when she came into her office to find the police commissioner sitting behind her desk.

He motioned her to sit down. Without further preamble, he began. "You know Beas, it's important that *outsiders* (He drew the word out) know they can't come into our house and fuck with us."

"Outsiders, Sir?"

"That's right. Who else? Because we're family, and family doesn't do that kind of thing."

He looked deeply into Whitfield eyes as if to hypnotize her. She just stared back blankly.

Inside, she was enraged. How dare he tell her how to conduct an investigation? This ridiculous political whore. He'd never been a real cop. He was just some ladder climber trying to get into office. He saw the police department as a vehicle for his political aspirations.

The commissioner got out of her chair and extended his hand. Whitfield took it and pressed lightly.

"Keep up the good work, Beas. Make those *outsiders* understand the true power of the NYPD." With that he left her office. Whitfield had the urge to spray disinfectant.

She sat at her desk trying not to scream obscenities at the walls. The door opened slightly, and Maisie walked in.

"Beas, none of us called that motherfucker. We're not really down with this whole dental thing, but we wouldn't rat you out. Dead ass."

Whitfield sighed heavily.

"Good, because I am going through with this."

Maisie nodded and left the office.

The process took two days, and it was stress filled the entire time. The quiet was so unsettling that Whitfield offered to bring in free pizza. They ate the pizza, but they were clearly tense.

The dentist, Dr. Lorie, did his job efficiently and thoroughly. Whitfield had been the first to have her saliva swabbed, and out of solidarity David had had his done too. A total of 15 detectives were swabbed. George kept a list and checked off everyone's name.

By mutual consent, it was decided not to discuss the results in Whitfield's office. The evidence would be sent by special courier and email.

"I'll send you the prints by email later on today. The courier should be here within the hour with the hard copies," Dr. Lorie said as he his assistants were packing up the equipment.

"Dr. Lorie," Whitfield said. "We appreciate your help and your discretion. . ."

"No problem."

George walked in casually, "I can go with Dr. Lorie and bring the records back", he offered.

Whitfield hadn't realized the office door was open. Still, she didn't want any courier. It was better to have her assistant bring the hard copies. She figured it would take an hour even in light traffic. Although had been his usual organized self, he had been withdrawn. It was good to see him back on board.

As a result, Whitfield was surprised when George didn't return. She called him, but there was no answer. When she checked her email, Dr. Lorie hadn't sent the print either.

The tests were a long shot, she knew, but they were also the best chance of isolating the killer. Whitfield was certain the killer was another cop.

"Doughnut run," David yelled from across the squad room.

Wolf whistles answered him, and Whitfield heard the stampede of cops getting free doughnuts.

Her husband pushed past the crowd of appreciative detectives and walked into his wife's office.

"I saved you a couple at the risk of limb and life." He said plopping a napkin full of delicious smelling pastry.

"Yummy, free my favorite," Whitfield with strained smile on her face.

"Actually, they *are* chocolate, but you clearly don't care one way or the other. What else is wrong?"

"The doc hasn't called with the prints, and George hasn't come back with the hard copies."

"Shit. What's up with that?"

"Don't know. I *do* know that I've called George, and he isn't answering his cell either."

David looked at her for a minute. She could almost hear him thinking that he never trusted George. This was important, and George was AWOL or something.

"Look," Whitfield said reining in her own worry about George. "As an assistant, George is very good and very reliable. Something could have happened to his phone. It's Sunday. Whatever it is, there's an explanation."

"Beas, there are public telephones. You can buy a trac phone for $10."

"Whatever," Whitfield said. "I need those prints, and now only I can go get them."

"I'll go with you." David offered.

"No, you're officially on leave. Remember?"

"But", David tried to interrupt.

"But nothing. You're not assigned to this case. You are a consultant. More like a volunteer really."

"And you can't go alone."

"No," Whitfield said emphatically. "I don't know why, but the vibe about this case is wrong. Until I hear from Dr. Lorie or George, nobody does anything on it alone. I'm taking Maisie."

"Beas, this is no ordinary cop killer. This is some kind of ghost."

"I don't believe in ghosts."

"You know what I mean," David said flexing his once-wounded arm. It was a nervous reaction whenever he felt uncomfortable.

"I mean no tracks, nothing," he said.

"We can use the tests." Whitfield said with conviction.

Before David could speak to that, Campbell walked into Whitfield's office. Tall and skinny, he looked like a teenager. Whitfield's secret name for him was "Anglo Saxon". His large blue eyes were trained on her.

"Chief, where's George?" He said getting right to the point.

"Don't know. That's not as important as the prints. The doc hasn't gotten back to me yet."

"I'll go and find out," Campbell said firmly.

"No, I'm going, and I'm taking Maisie."

"Chief, I'm volunteering", Campbell was a man on a mission.

Whitfield's cell phone rang. It was Jamie.

"I know the word Uncle Glenn was trying to say." She began breathlessly. "He said the name is Doughnuts."

"Doughnuts? That's food." Whitfield asked.

"No, not food. He said it like it was a name. "

"Okay. Thanks. You've done something very important Jamie. I'll be in touch."

"Soon?"

"Definitely."

She said goodbye and hung up. Whitfield blinked as if that would clear her mind.

Turning her attention to Campbell, she imagined him in her position in about 15 years. Anglo Saxon was police chief material. Damn, she thought he was police commissioner material. He was intelligent and a little reckless. Whitfield blamed the latter trait on youth. He had integrity and grit.

She had liked him immediately, but didn't want to show that. Favoritism was anathema in a police department. Worse, it created envy and back stabbing. Whitfield had seen it before. Yet, Campbell was right. He was there, and he was volunteering. There would be other assignments for Maisie.

"Fine." She glanced at David.

She glanced at her husband. Without admitting that she had changed her mind, she said,

"Detective Whitfield is coming along as a consultant."

David blinked in surprise but quickly recovered his composure. Campbell nodded to David and stepped aside to let Whitfield pass. The ride there was uneventful except the police radio seemed to be on the fritz. Whitfield assumed the murders had put even the mechanics in the garage on edge. The radio had probably been overlooked.

The dental school was located in an old municipal building. It was late Sunday, and the building was closed. As with all buildings of New York City, there was 24 hour 7 day a week security. Except, there were none. The building looked totally empty. Whitfield rang the night bell. Campbell tried pushing the revolving door and found it unlocked. The other doors were also unlocked.

"Something is wrong", Campbell voiced what each of them was thinking.

All three of them pulled their guns. Whitfield led them into the building. David and Campbell flanked her.

"Hello", she called. The building was neo-roman with high vaulted ceilings. The floors were marble, and the building was granite. It was like a man-made mountain. Her voice echoed around the large chamber. They walked slowly into the reception desk. The lights on the console were off.

"Where are the guards?" She said. "They must be here."

"They are," Campbell looking at the ceiling where he stood.

Hanging from the dome like human mobiles were the bodies of three men. From where Whitfield stood, they seemed to be facing one another. Each of them was the same blue-white as the three cops killed in the precinct. None of them was as fat as those cops, but all of them looked muscular.

They must have been hired right out of the army, Whitfield thought. These men were soldiers. How could they have been hanged?

"No blood," David said looking around the desk, under the desk, on the desk. They all looked everywhere. Blood on a marble floor would be impossible to conceal.

"Call this in," she said looking at Campbell.

"The killer is OCD." David responded matter-of-factly. "Looked how evenly the bodies are spaced."

"They're responding, Chief," Campbell said.

He stared at the ceiling again.

"What is it Campbell?" "Something about that mural," he said. "It looks wacky."

"David," Whitfield said turning to her husband. "Did you bring your binoculars?

In answer, he reached into his coat pocket and pulled out a pair of small field glasses. He walked over to the spot directly beneath the mural and looked.

"This is why Dr. Lorie didn't answer the phone." He said holding the binoculars out to his wife.

She looked up and saw the head of Dr. Lorie impaled on one of the figures of the mural.

She handed the glasses to Campbell.

"What the fuck! He said.

"We've got to find George, and the rest of Dr. Lorie."

"Chief this has to be more than one guy." Campbell said.

He's trying to master his fear, Whitfield. Good for him. I hope I can master mine. This was a fresh new hell.

Still flanked by David and Campbell, Whitfield turned on the console and found Dr. Lorie's office.

"Stairs," she said.

"How many flights?" her husband asked.

"Two".

"Wait," Campbell said. He picked up a shotgun from behind the desk and offered it to Whitfield.

She shook her head. Following his lead, she checked for automatic weapons. There was a small one, a flame thrower and an axe.

"What were they preparing for a wooden homicidal maniac?" She said looking at David.

He shrugged his shoulders and took the flame thrower. Whitfield took the assault rifle, and the three headed up the stairs.

They were quiet and Whitfield could hear the slow even breaths of her husband contrasted to the short nervous breathing of Campbell.

On the second floor, they continued in their formation. They walked into Dr. Lorie's office, where a young woman was slumped over a desk. She looked Asian. The nameplate on her desk read Wu Lin, assistant coroner. Campbell checked her pulse and shook his head.

They walked into Dr. Lorie's office. There was no sign of him. A closet door opened and George walked out. His eyes were blazing, and he looked feverish with sweat.

Whitfield recognized shock when she saw it.

"Easy George. You're in shock." George was swallowing hard. His hands were blood soaked.

David walked toward George. As he advanced, George began to giggle. Then he laughed. Then he guffawed loudly. Campbell shook his head again.

Whitfield said, "George, we're taking you down for observation. There's no shame in being afraid. If hiding in the closet saved your life, that's a good thing."

George stopped laughing abruptly and hissed. David hadn't moved any farther, but he looked warily at George.

There was a loud thump, and the body of Dr. Lorie fell out of the closet. David made a move to check Dr. Lorie, but George blocked him.

"He's gone," George said firmly.

"Move George," David said motioning with his hand.

"I'm not really George," George said licking his hands.

"George, you're obstructing police business." Whitfield said.

George gave her the finger and nimbly leapt onto Dr. Lorie's desk. With the agility of a gymnast, he back flipped out of the window behind it. The three of them rushed over to the window.

Whitfield was certain she would see George's body splayed out on the pavement. Instead, she saw him running confidently across the parking lot. Clearly, he had hit the ground running and seemed to be unhurt. The insane could run incredibly fast, Whitfield knew.

"George, stop. We can help you." Campbell shouted.

"What the fuck happened?" David said. "Did George pretend to be dead and hide in the closet?"

Whitfield sighed. There was no other explanation she could think of.

They heard men running into the building. Her walkie-talkie squawked.

"Chief, where are you?"

"We're on the second floor. We think the place is empty, but proceed with extreme caution. There may be several preps here."

"Copy."

"Yeah."

Campbell had been looking out of the window next to them. He shook his head stubbornly. "Fuck. Look at Doughnuts go. That's some Olympic shit there."

"What did you call him?" Whitfield said with a sinking feeling in her stomach.

"Doughnuts. We call him that because he's always eating them. Leaving powder and crumbs all over the place. The man is a pig. What... why are you guys looking at me like that?'"

Whitfield didn't bother to answer. She got on the walkie-talkie.

"Don't bother covering the building. We're fine. I want the area within a mile radius covered. You're looking for Police Officer George Hesub. He is in uniform. A male white, 6'1'', light brown hair, crew cut. The suspect is dangerous. Very possibly psychotic." She could hear footsteps running down the hall toward the office. Then the footsteps stopped."

"Copy that chief." It sounded like MacNally was responding to her orders. A few moments later, she looked out of the window and saw the cops pour out of the building into the surrounding area.

"Does he have the records?" She asked just to break the weird feeling she had.

"I didn't see anything in his hand," Campbell offered. Then added, "Except..." His voice trailed off.

"Blood", David finished.

Author Interviews - Loretta H. Campbell

Hi, Loretta H. Campbell!

What was your inspiration for this story?
I have always loved horror stories. That's why I write them. Moreover, I like the idea of portraying cops as vampires. I live in New York City, and the number of Black people killed by police officers seems to increase every year. It feels like they are supernatural assassins. I wrote the story in support of all the Black people who have been the innocent victims of police officers. I entered this story in a horror story contest. It was not accepted, but I believed then and now, that it's a good story. I found Black Girl Magic Literary Magazine through the Brian Scott Morning Coffee Newsletter. Thank you for accepting my short story.

Why did you choose a Black woman as your main character?
Like all lovers of literature, I want to see myself in the fiction that I read. That seldom happens. I want to be part of the solution in writing Black women into literature.

Why did you want to submit to Black Girl Magic Lit Mag?
I was so excited when I found a publication of Black and for Black women that focuses on horror and speculative fiction. I couldn't wait to be a part of it! I hope you have T-shirts because I want to wear one.

What are your favorite novels or short stories?

My favorite novel is *The Master and Margarita* by Mikhail Bulgakov (the Mirra Ginsburg translation). I like it because it's an extraordinary mixture of satire, science fiction, and horror. Here was a Russian, in the early 1900s, who trounced organized religion, communism, and death. You have to admire that kind of courage. I'm religious, but I think he was a wonderful writer. My other favorite novels are The *Blacksmith's Daughter* by Minnette Coleman. This is so well written. It has the kind of texture and depth that makes you feel completely sated after reading it. I had the pleasure of hearing Ms. Coleman read an excerpt. I can't recommend it highly enough. All of Octavia E. Butler's books are my favorites. My favorite favorite is *Survivor*. I love her short stories from *Bloodchild and Other Stories*. I think her characters are people that I see everyday. They are just that real. I interviewed her once. Unfortunately, I couldn't find a publisher for the piece. I have the hard copy of the interview still. She told me that she got her ideas from reading science magazines. I find that amazing. She also told me that she hated Survivor. That's just wrong, in my opinion. However, she wrote the novel, so there you go. The Mill on the Floss by George Eliot is another of my favorites. I have read most of her novels. It's still the one that I return to time and again. Zone One by Colson Whitehead takes horror in another direction, I think. The pace is glacial but riveting and frightening. The vocabulary is stunning. All of these things won me over. "Afterward", the short story by Edith Wharton is, to my mind, the perfect ghost story. The irony in it knocks me out. Sister Carrie by Theodore Dreiser is a great novel because of its verisimilitude. Dreiser was not afraid to simply tell the truth. It reads beautifully. I have the urge to say "You go girl" whenever I read it. *Up Above My Head* is one of my favorites by James Baldwin. He has such compassion and love for Black people. It comes through every line of all his work. I think he was a very loving and great spirited man too. Of course, his craft was exemplary. Song of Solomon by Toni Morrison is triumphant and gritty. That's why I love it. She is fearless in her depiction of our lives. Her work makes me want to stand up straight and throw my shoulders back. Her characters embody the pride--the justifiable pride of Black people. *Plague of Doves* and *Love Medicine* are novels by Louise Erdrich. All of her writing is cinematic to me. She has a way of making passion seem like an addiction. Frankly, I think it is. Her short story "American Horse" is gut wrenching. It reads like the unwritten history of America. Joyce Carol Oates's story, "Where Are You Going Where Have You Been" is so precise that it's tactile. It is one of the most disturbing stories that I've ever read. I've read it a lot. The early short stories of Erskine Caldwell are a treasure trove. I really admire the way he captures the cadence and attitude of various socio-economic classes. It's as if he has exposed the decaying roots of a very old tree. I subscribe to Maya Angelou's advice about being catholic in the reading. I read mostly fiction, but I also read non-fiction. I regret that I only read one language. I intend to rectify that though.

Tell us something about your future writing endeavors?
About 20 years ago, I worked for a newspaper in Brooklyn, NY called The City Sun. Because of that work, I learned the true value of deadlines. Also because of that work, I need deadlines to finish a short story. I can procrastinate until the world falls off its axis. So, my future projects include submitting my short stories to publications with deadlines. These deadlines have to be within a month off. Otherwise, I will just daydream and not do anything. I had given serious thought and effort to starting a business creating coloring books of my short stories. The truth is, all I want to do is write and submit the work. I had an idea to write a cookbook, but nothing grips me like just writing fiction, horror, or science fiction, or something like those two genres. This is a long winded way of saying my future projects are just to write every weekday morning and submit--often.

World of Rain: Adaeze's Ambition - Miri Castor

My home is here. Adaeze Durgakama giggled as she hugged her chubby, deep sienna-skinned arms. Squeezed in the corner of the smog-filled study, Adaeze rocked herself as she laughed at the thought. *My home is here now.*

Her maroon-tinted body felt like it was floating over the unkempt floor, with diagrams, incomplete chemical formulas, and notes she had taken from her classes at the institution she attended. Nicaian bubbled sporadically in the bottle beside her feet; it was the same substance that had submersed Adaeze's brain under its influence, the same substance that was coursing through her body, the same substance that made her feel like she truly had a Gift, as it granted the maown—the Earth term was "woman"—in her twenty-first year the wonderful illusion of hovering. "*My home is here,*" repeated Adaeze aloud, covering her mouth as she burst into a laughing fit. ""What will Maj say?"

Rudo Durgakama would not be pleased, she was the older maown who pushed Adaeze out of her uterus years ago,—Adaeze couldn't recall the exact number in this euphoric state. Adaeze's own maj, she would only have one of those…unless it was possible for multiple maown to give birth to doppelgangers of an Athrenian, each carrying a piece of a genetic identity that made up a whole Athrenian.

Adaeze snickered as three maown appeared before her. She recognized one of them as her maj, her skin as dark as the gaping night sky with a magenta tint. The intensity of Rudo's auburn eyes made Adaeze chuckle. *Smile, Maj. Is it possible for you to smile at me,* wondered Adaeze. The other maown were similar to her maj, with wide hips and robust thighs. But their skin was sepia colored, with brighter shades of red undertones. The doppelgangers shared a common characteristic, their scowl.

I have no imagination. I can't help it, that is how Maj looks at me.

Adaeze tittered more, slamming her hand against the floor. It took her a moment to realize that she was pounding the diagrams she drew in class, crinkling her meticulous notes on neoglycolysis, the process in which Athrenians converted lucose into useable energy. Her enraptured state left her as Adaeze panted, a greyish blue plume leaving her with every breath. Nicaian was doing its work, interfering with the body's metabolism, and transporting the lezymes that catalyzed the inhibition of regulatory proteins—this made her muscles tense, her breath fast, her thoughts scattered, and her memories vivid. As her head slumped back against the wall and her braids cascaded past her shoulders, Adaeze's body went limp. Sleep was the Athrenian's defense mechanism against nicaian when it reached this point of intensity.

She could hear a maown's voice, a trembling voice that lacked any fortitude. An angry, tender voice that wasn't supposed to sound like this. "We could've had a home away from all of this. But you've…you made up your mind, Addy. This is your home now."

"Addy". The pubescent voice brought her back from the agonizing memory.

Adaeze opened her eyes and began to process where she was. She cleared her throat and rose to her feet, peering out the window. Her cracked feet crushed the scattered papers across the dinky, muggy room. The colorless sun shone like a jewel in the pale mauve sky; District 8's aesthetics did not change overnight. The shacks in the distance appeared to be barely standing, trash swarmed the floating walkways ripped from the ground. Red orbs of bacteria were scattered across the walkways.

"Are you prepared?" asked Adaeze, turning away from the window to face Evron Moreno, the boy who woke her.

Evron weakly kicked up some papers, then nodded. His taupe eyes fell to the floor, the boy still wasn't used to seeing Adaeze in a cropped cami and shorts. *He is young,* thought Adaeze humorously. He then pinched his nose, the lingering, pungent scent of nicaian must have been harsh on his olfactory senses. She softly chuckled as she gathered her thin braids over her left shoulder, putting them into one large braid. "Let us speak in a moment," said Adaeze.

Evron stepped back and closed the door with a sulky look; Adaeze braided the smaller braids over her other shoulder with a tired sigh.

She left her study fully dressed. Adaeze was fortunate to have Evron leave her washed clothes in her study instead of in her bedroom. She rarely used it; she wore a simple, dark olive poncho and black pants of stretchy material for comfort, repelling rainwater, and running. Adaeze hurried down the hall, the floor creaking with every step. She lowered her head as the ceiling sloped, with Evron was waiting for her at the bottom of the steps.

"Did you contact Anza?" Adaeze spoke sternly as she jogged down the steps. She pressed her hand against the wall, the dim lights that she had put up herself faintly illuminated the stairwell.

"Yeah, she's bringing the Charm today", answered Evron. "She's takin' so long. We need to get the new Charm started on training."

Adaeze reached the bottom, briefly gazing at the dim chamber. The pit was empty, their "pet snake"—Evron used this endearing term—was nowhere to be seen. Adaeze had hoped it would be here with the coming of Opal Charm, the human Adaeze needed.

"You don't trust your friend?" asked Adaeze mischievously.

"Ai! Never said that," replied a flustered Evron. "She's been messing ''round too much on Earth, I think. Gettin' caught up in that horrible place."

Adaeze looked to the olive-skinned boy. He wore a disgruntled expression, which was a part of his normal, irritable demeanor. *I was a happier child than him.* She wondered if the majority of Earth males who were in their fourteenth years were like Evron. Adaeze dismissed the thought, she had an important plan to keep on schedule today. Still, she couldn't help but entertain herself. "Earth is your home, is it not?"

Evron crossed his veiny arms as he lowered his eyes. "Yeah."

"Yet, you show much disdain for it."

Evron couldn't respond, Adaeze knew he wouldn't. She chuckled—the young boy was a reflection of herself. "This is your home now", reminded Adaeze with a hint of scorn. Her earnest tone returned, "We are leaving now. District 27 is where JAEL will establish itself as an organization against Samael." If she said it enough times, Adaeze would begin to believe it. After all the work they had done in the past four years, it all amounted to nothing now.

JAEL was group Adaeze founded, she was its maj—a Justice Allegiance for Every Lusan. It was created to eliminate the Khan Serkhan, the ruler of the districts and Lusa. Samael was overextending his power, Adaeze knew he would; bathing in the Fountain of Youth and becoming immortal was not enough to satisfy his insatiable thirst for power. He would conquer the entire world of Athre and then......do what? Create a world for Gifted Athrenians? Find the world Adaeze was desperate to keep hidden from him—Earth? *He would ruin that world, as he is doing to this one,* answered Adaeze her own question.

The members of JAEL were the only ones who knew of Earth and its importance. It was the home of not only Evron, but the Charm family—the only people capable of killing Samael and stopping whatever plans he had. With the exception of Evron, the Charms were the only humans with Gifts. Gifts that could usurp temporal and spatial rules, and arrogate the laws that governed life and death that Athrenians were forced to live with. *Humans, too, for that matter,* added Adaeze.

Currently, the youngest family member was Adaeze's last resort. Opal Charm, a female human in her thirteenth year…she was quite young. But youth could not interfere with the task of defeating Samael, and saving Athre and Earth. Adaeze was young when she decided to take on Samael herself, organize JAEL, leave her maj's home, fall in love, and break her own heart.

Her thoughts lurched to Lavanda, the maown that Adaeze used to break her heart. Before Adaeze allowed herself to be submerged in the wonderful memories of the beautiful Athrenian, she remembered her last words to Adaeze, *"This is your home, now"*.

Adaeze's heart sank, and then remembered—she didn't have one. She had keep saying it until she believed it.

"Addy, are we going or what?" asked Evron impatiently.

Adaeze went into the adjacent stairwell and hurried to the upper floor. As her eyes fell on the dim lights, the cold steps, and finally, the trapdoor over her head, Lavanda's image haunted her. A fat maown with plump arms and thighs, russet skin with an undertone of lilac. Eyes the color of reddish-brown onyx and curly hair that matched Adaeze's eyes. Lavanda smelled of sardoffils, "flowers" was what humans would say. Adaeze didn't know enough about Earth's flowers to distinguish one and compare the scents—she only knew that sardoffils were the sweetest smelling "flower" that existed on Lusa.

She turned halfway around in the stairwell after opening the trapdoor. "Let's make haste."

***

District 27 flourished with Lusans. It was of the fourteenth hour, the hour in which Lusans spent leisure time in Roi Metropolis. Evron called it "a park", most likely because of the lush verdure, the trees, and the Waking Meadow adjacent to it. Waking Meadow, the Meadow was the common name, was an empty field that was free of the anti-gravitational forces that were set in place across the world. Gravitas Delunarius mediated the force of gravity, allowing Athrenians who were outdoors and other places to float above the ground. Athrenians like Adaeze used the hovering walkways—"sidewalks" Evron called them—as a directional guide, showing where people couldn't and could hover-walk.

Adaeze pushed down on her black sunhat as she lowered her head. Evron was dressed in clothes Lasperanza, their fellow JAEL member, purchased for him—a brown, loose-fitting shirt and black pants similar to Adaeze's. Her thighs brushed each other as Adaeze strolled toward the brass statue of Samael, a magnificent showcase of the adolescent tyrant with his hands raised to the sky. Sardoffils and rosemars, another type of "flower", surrounded the base of the statue; Lusa's perpetual drizzle kept them well nourished. Lusans in their twentieth years were leaned against statue waiting, speaking to others, and interlocked in each other's arms as they laid in the bed of sardoffils and rosemars. Adaeze couldn't help but envision her and Lavanda doing the latter. It didn't help that the scent of sardoffils was strong.

"Let us do this quickly and discretely," said Adaeze, turning to Evron.

"Got it."

Evron will utilize his spatial Gift and catalyze the decomposition of this statue. By the time we return to District 8, the statue will start decomposing. An announcement will air, the statue would be broadcasted across most districts. District 28 and above will not hear about it, but any exposure helps.
The plan remained unchanged in Adaeze's mind; she watched Evron squat in front of the statue's plaque. Dark violet matter seeped from his fingertips and permeated the plaque. She stood beside him, pretending to observe the sardoffils. To affirm her cover as a plant scientist, she mumbled questions to Evron regarding the plants. He was ignoring her and concentrating on his work, as Adaeze needed him to be.

She was envious of Evron's Gift. It allowed him to distort gravity, moderately catalyze the destruction of matter, and possibly reconstruct it if he knew how to properly utilize his Gift. Most importantly, Evron could traverse between Athre and Earth; Adaeze could detect the presence of Gifts through physical contact. It was a miniscule Gift, a joke in a world where people could fly, exhale flames, and merge with matter. Even on Earth it was a joke, the presence of the Charm family ensured that.

Twilight was an exclusive Gift for members of the Charm family, an unnatural Gift that varied with each Charm member. It was a Gift that came in a pair—there was a Charm's primary Gift and secondary Gift. Twilight was always the primary Gift that enhanced the capabilities of the secondary Gift. Based on what Lasperanza told her regarding Opal Charm, Adaeze could not discern what Opal's secondary Gift was.

Adaeze turned away from the sardoffils and glanced at Evron. He was doing what needed to be done—what? Adaeze's eyes narrowed as she scrutinized Evron's furious expression, then his hands. Plumes of violet poured from them as the foundation of the statue darkened at an incredible rate. "What're you doing?" demanded Adaeze, covering his backside. She was tall and her chubby thighs shielded Evron appropriately.

He didn't respond, furrowing his thick eyebrows as he curled his fingers. None of the Lusans seemed aware that he was causing it, but Adaeze noticed a few staring in their general direction. Adaeze was starting to get vex as she waited for an answer.

"I'm doing what you wanted", seethed Evron.

"Which is what?"

She didn't have to wait for his answer. The brass statue quickly became drained of color. Adaeze couldn't have ever imagined Evron's Gift was capable of extremely rapid decomposition. She should've realized sooner—she knew his anger was the primary source of energy for his Gift. What was in his thoughts that angered him so?

Adaeze didn't have time to wonder. She pulled Evron away from the statue of Samael and sped-walked through Roi Metropolis. Curious Lusans began to clamor around the degrading statue, fear coiled around her chest as she anticipated what would happen next. Evron walked beside her, trying to conceal his angry expression. Adaeze always knew there was a risk of Evron straying away from her plans, his temperamental disposition as a fourteenth year confirmed the risk. Murmurs and gasps filled the crowd, Adaeze started to jog while Evron broke into a sprint. She turned around and watched the statue become engulfed in a dark violet hue; she bumped into what felt like a child as she sped out of the crowd. "The hell's wrong with you people?" The voice belonged to a boy, but Adaeze paid no mind to him.

"I never said to blow it up," snapped Adaeze, putting her hand on her hat. She tried to steady her voice in a quiet tone, but frustration amplified it. "What're you thinking?"

Evron stopped, his fists clenched. The anger he had melted away, his tone was urgent, "I'm thinkin' it's time to make a statement".

"Fuckin' pricks!" The same voice that yelled at them the first time was louder. She stole a glance at the boy, a light copper-skinned thirteenth or fourteenth year with monolid eyes filled with rage. Adaeze gave Evron a look that said, "Do not fight anyone. We have to leave immediately."

Evron obeyed the unspoken command as Adaeze sped off, heading in the direction of District 8. She could see the boy chasing them in her peripheral vision. As Adaeze predicted, an explosion erupted behind them, the statue of Samael would cease to exist. She could only imagine how the statue looked—engulfed in flames, smoke darker than residual nicaian blanketing a piece of the sky. Horrified screams filled the entire district.

"Why's this guy following us!?" cried Evron, hustling beside Adaeze.

She turned a corner, entering the domestic zone of District 26. The houses here were in decent shape compared to the decrepit shacks in District 8. Anything looked better than District 8—and that was how Adaeze hoped it would stay. District 8 was the most unsuspecting district, no Khan would think that a group like JAEL would have their base set up there.

Nosy Lusans whished by as Adaeze and Evron ran away from the explosion. If the boy didn't stop chasing them, Adaeze would have to incapacitate him.

"Just let 'em go!"

A girl's voice, sounding as if she was in her twelve or thirteen year, appeared behind Adaeze. "That was really stupid Aaron—what would've happened if I couldn't find you?"

Adaeze began to slow down, she saw that the boy stopped chasing them. His glare on her and Evron only became more intensive. "Who do you pricks think you are, huh?"

Evron will accept the challenge, assumed Adaeze. She
saw Evron come to a halt, anger flashing across his face.
Adaeze knew what would happen next—he would charge over
there and beat both of them. She couldn't allow that, they were
everyday Lusans; she snatched his arm as he tried whirling
around to face the pursuer.

"What d'you say?" called Evron, his nostrils flaring.

"Stop it now," whispered Adaeze without any leniency.

With the bony-armed girl pulling on her associate, the
casually dressed boy advanced toward them. Adaeze pulled her
sunhat down while observing the young Lusans attire; his loose
shirt had an animal's face on it, accompanied by the words,
Pugs not Drugs and long, soft looking pants fit for slumber.
The girl was dressed in similar nightwear, wearing a sleeveless
shirt that revealed thin arms. *Curious Lusans,* observed Adaeze.
They lacked a color tint on their skin, unlike the vast majority
of brownish colored Lusans.

The girl had dark umber skin, her deep brown hair lied
in a realm between straight and voluminous. Most dark-skinned
Lusans didn't straighten her hair like this one had, the Lusan
drizzle reverted their straightened hair to thick curls.

"Aaron, please calm down." The girl sounded fearful—
she should have been. She didn't know what either of them
were capable of. "Please not now. Come on."

Where have I seen her before? Adaeze kept her hand
clasped around Evron's arm as he tried shaking out of her
grasp. The boy with monolid eyes relaxed his muscles,
seemingly calm.

"Sorry. I'm really…" the boy called Aaron was
mumbling to the girl, wiping his face with his shirt. "I'm…ugh,
sorry. I didn't even realize that I—"

"It's okay, idiot." The girl weakly smiled at him, then
turned to Adaeze and Evron. Adaeze watched Evron's anger
dissipate as the girl gazed at the two of them fearfully. She
released his arm, waiting to hear whatever the girl had to say.
"We're really sorry."

There was no longer anything to worry about. The young Lusans didn't see them blow up the statue, there would be no need for violence. Adaeze and Evron exchanged glances and ran back towards District 8. When she couldn't see them anymore, Evron let out a fatigued sigh with his hands behind his head. "What was that about?"

"Foolish Lusans in their thirteenths," figured Adaeze. She wasn't letting Evron avoid the matter at hand—he deviated from her plan and blew up a statue. They were forced to flee conspicuously; Adaeze wanted JAEL to be recognized, but not as a terror group. "What you did was violently horrendous, Evron."

Evron sucked his teeth.

"This attitude of yours will hinder our plans", scolded Adaeze. Evron's head sunk, her words finally resonated with him. ""How can we fight Samael if we hurt other Lusans in the process? We are supposed to bring Lusans to our side without the threat of violence. I am not a fool, I know violence is necessary for stopping Samael…, but there was no need for what you did."

"I hate…"

"Repeat yourself."

"I hate him."

Adaeze chuckled bitterly. "You haven't met Samuel. Your hatred of him is illogical."

"I hate him for what he did to this place. Lo matería," muttered Evron darkly.

The source of Evron's hatred for Samael and Earth was still a mystery after knowing him for many years. Adaeze had justified reasons for hating her home and Samael, Evron was an outsider. A boy who permanently moved from his home world, Earth, to Athre. When Adaeze had asked him about it, he would reply angrily, *He ruined this world.* It was as if he had a resolute, idealized image of Lusa before Samael's rule. It was unlikely that Evron came here when Lusa was in an aesthetic, rudimentary state.

"You two, wait!"

The voice of the girl stopped Adaeze and Evron in their tracks. She could see the worry and tenseness behind Evron's fury. Why was this girl bothering them?

"What?" asked Adaeze curtly. The girl was panting heavily, as if she ran locomiles to catch them. "Is there an issue?""

"Y-yes," stammered the girl.

"What the hell? What's goin' on?" The girl's friend caught up to them hastily. Adaeze could picture both of them hunched over as she gave them her back. Her face couldn't be seen by potential threats, even if they were young Lusans. Evron glared at the girl closest to Adaeze.

"Here for a fight?" threatened Evron. Adaeze grabbed his arm firmly, preventing him from making any sudden moves.

"Stop," hissed Adaeze, silencing Evron. Then she asked the young Lusan brusquely, "What is your qualm?"

When the girl didn't immediately reply, Adaeze conjured a believable lie. "If you have none, let us be on our way. We have to take shelter from the bomb's noxious fumes.""

Adaeze waited for the girl's reply, she seemed at a loss for words. She stole a glance at the young girl, watching her look to her friend for support. "We will not be stalled here," stated Adaeze. She pulled on Evron's arm as they began to hover-walk away.

"Y-you guys did that, right?" shouted the girl.

What a foolish girl, griped Adaeze. Evron jumped in her grasp.

"Did what?" yelled Evron.

"The bomb. You guys did it," stuttered the girl fretfully.

Adaeze released Evron as he sneered at the untinted Lusan. *A brash young Lusan. I used to be like that.* Adaeze chuckled as remembered yelling at one of her leading scientists in her laboratory. She had been pointing at the Khan accusingly while her free hand was gripping Lavanda's hand. Adaeze couldn't remember at the moment why she was yelling at the Khan, but she remembered she was fuming—more importantly, Lavanda was at her side, squeezing her hand and smiling at her.

Adaeze felt like entertaining the girl before she would let Evron handle her. She lowered her head, "You're assuming we had something to do with the explosion?"

If the Lusan was smart, she would lie.

"Y-yeah," replied the Lusan. "You took off before it happened, that's how I know you two are the ones who did it. An' I heard you talkin' about it."

Adaeze had to see this foolish Lusan again, before Evron had his way. She turned halfway around, seeing the girl step farther away from her warily. The air of familiarity struck Adaeze once more, she definitely met this girl before. Not by her home, and not on the Sonny Tram—Lusa's main transportation system—Adaeze had no recollection of meeting her anywhere in Lusa.

"And now what?" derided Adaeze, chuckling softly. Familiar or not, she would not let this girl expose them. "I take it you didn't plan ahead for this. Now what will you and your friend do?"

The initial pursuer, Aaron, came up behind the frightened girl. "We gotta go," he told her urgently. They should've left sooner.

Evron shook his arms out, displaying mannerisms that indicated he would be fighting soon. He stepped toward them. "Taking the coward's way out now, huh? What was pointin' us out going to prove?"

"Woah, c'mon now," muttered Aaron anxiously, his palms raised. This would only provoke Evron. Adaeze thought they were too young to be killed, the friends were close in age to Evron. However, allowing them to run away would be a hazard.

"I think their elimination is necessary," said Adaeze to Evron, giving him permission to do as he pleased. Horror welled up the girl's dark hazel eyes as tears——wait. Hazel eyes of that hue were uncommon, Adaeze wondered where she was truly from. She suppressed her curiosity, the young Lusans would die soon. "You should have let us walk away."

Aaron scurried in front of his friend, a noble act of concern for her. Adaeze admired it, but it wasn't stopping Evron as he drew nearer to them.

"She-she's really sorry, we're sorry. We are so very sorry, we won't tell anyone what you did," promised a high strung Aaron. "We're lost, we're actually very lost!"

They were lost? That accounted for their sleepwear.

Evron grabbed Aaron's shirt and lifted him up with ease, his gravity-tempering Gift eliminated objects' pull of gravity downward. The girl hurried to Evron's side, another unwise decision on her part. "He-he's right!" she added, her voice trembling. "We just came from another world—"

"Do you take us for morons?" Evron cried out. A surge of anxiety overcame Adaeze as she pondered the possibility. *She said the two of them came from another world. Not any other place like Lusa or Gardaia. Is it merely a matter of strange word choice?* Adaeze had to wonder. As she began to consider the girl's statement, the girl bravely, but senselessly grabbed Evron's raised fist, stopping him from punching Aaron. Evron sputtered, ""I'll kill you, too."

He wouldn't. Adaeze knew he wouldn't kill anyone. He threatened, he yelled, he displayed aggressive mannerisms, but he was a fearful fourteenth year. Nonetheless, she kept watching; any remaining Lusans nearby had already left for Roi Metropolis, leaving Adaeze and the others alone in this desolate street.

"Opal, back off!" cried Aaron, wincing as he awaited Evron's fist. "Get the hell outta here."

"I'm not leaving you, Aaron."

Opal? That was her name. It was like a splash of cold water on her sleeping memory cells. Adaeze gasped as she began to understand why the girl was so intriguing to observe. This girl named "Opal" was not a Lusan. She was not even Athrenian.

If Adaeze's hunch was correct, which she felt was, this was the girl that was in her tenth year who Adaeze spoke to on Earth three years ago. She met her at her a funeral, the girl had wanted her funeral ornament on top of the buried urn. After reading her palms, Adaeze had assured the tenth year of a bright future…the girl that lacked any Gift, but had the surname of great importance—Charm. Was this strange girl the same one they were supposed to bring to Lusa? The same one Adaeze spent years monitoring?

Adaeze refocused on the scene unfolding. Evron pushed Opal into the floating street and Aaron was now standing straight, fecklessly watching her. Evron's demeanor conveyed to Adaeze he was going get extremely violent soon, she couldn't allow this to continue. There was a strong possibility that they had been waiting for this girl.

Adaeze hurried to Evron and gripped his shoulder. She gave him a stern look, a look that left no room for argument. He relaxed his fists, returning the serious countenance. Adaeze knew he could tell something was off, he knew not to argue with her. She looked up at Opal, sitting stiffly as she met Adaeze's eyes. Opal's hands were on the invisible, anti-gravitational barrier—it was an unnecessary act. The barrier would hold her up, regardless of where she placed her hands; Adaeze's hunch that the girl was the human named Opal Charm grew stronger.

"What is your full name?" inquired Adaeze earnestly. She stole a glance at Aaron gaping at Opal as she remained seated above the street.

"Huh?" stuttered Opal. She was on the brink of tears.

Do not go dumb. I am trying to help you.

Adaeze folded her arms. "Your name?"

The girl sniveled and replied timidly; Adaeze listened as if the girl was addressing all of Lusa, "O-Opal. Opal Charm."

Honey hazel eyes were the distinctive trait of the Charm members. Those eyes bounced between Evron and Adaeze; Adaeze tried to force down her joy. Her heart fluttered as she covered her mouth and lowered her head behind Evron, concealing her smile. The dreams of defeating Samael, of ruining the Khan system Samael established, and returning home resurfaced from the depths of her heart. Being in Lavanda's arms and the scent of sardoffils engulfed Adaeze's senses—the human that would make that all possible, the girl who now carried the wondrous Gift of Twilight, the girl of thirteenth year who took the Path of Dawn and Dusk sat dumbfounded in front of Adaeze, her name Opal Charm.

About Miri Castor

Miri Castor is the author of the Opal Charm urban fantasy series. She spent many recesses in middle school writing fantasy stories, with The Path to Dawn being one of many. She has written for Black Girl Magic Literary Magazine and was featured as a Spotlight New Author in January 2016. Now attending a university on the East Coast, she studies biochemistry and will receive her B.S. in 2016. A New York native, Miri is working on her second novel while in her last year as an undergraduate. She enjoys playing video games, attending music concerts, and strolling through the city.

https://twitter.com/charmedcastor
http://miricastor.tumblr.com/

Sisters - Jacqueline Nicole Harris

When we had finished making love, I thought I saw a shadow move across our room just before the lights came on. And when they did come on, she was there standing by the foot of the bed with a look of triumph on her face. A look that should have been mine.

Here I was, in her bed, under her roof, making love to Darren and all she could do was smile like that. This was supposed to be my moment. This was supposed to be our time.

"Turn off the light please." I giggled coyly. "We are not done yet."

"Oh really," said my sister.

Yes. She was/is my twin sister. Alike in every way except one: She can't fuck, but I can. She lacked the skills to satisfy him. But he knew that.

"Is mommy's favorite going to have a temper tantrum now?"

"No darling", she spit. "But I think you are going to scream for me."

Darren said nothing. He never says anything. Darren remained silent and frozen with a bemused look on his face. He would say that every time she caught us, our ensuing catfights turned him on. I must admit they turned me on too. But this time was different. This time there would be no hot catfight for us to fuck about later.

This time she grabs me by my arms like she is going to pull me from him. No chance in hell I thought, as she kept that stupid grin on her face. Her grip got tighter and tighter. Her fingernails dug deeper and deeper into my flesh and my arms started to bleed.

She had said something to us about screaming, I was not going to give her the satisfaction. But, then Darren started to shout, "Alright, let her go!"
I gritted my teeth and hissed at my sister. I could feel the wounds in my arms burning, burning like hell fire.

Darren tried hitting her; smacking her across the shoulders and the head. She still wouldn't let go. The look of twisted glee on her face mirrored the agony that I felt. I couldn't take anymore.

"Scream for me sister! Scream!"

I screamed.

"Baby, wake up!"

I awake sopping wet with sweat and chilled to the bone.

"You were having that nightmare again. Damn baby!"

"It was my sister," I say.

"It's all in your mind," He says pausing to yawn for minute, before stretching, and rolling out of bed scratching his butt.

"You don't even have a sister," He says.

"What do you know," I think to myself. *What do you know?*

It was a cold night in Zion. The nightmare was still fresh in my mind. So much so that when he left the room, I got on my knees to pray. The words, my God, the words got stuck in my throat again.

I got off of my knees quickly when I heard Darren coming back. I opened the bedroom window. Our front yard was covered in a blanket of snow that glittered like diamonds under the moonlight. I stood there breathing in the cold.

He says I am letting the heat out.

"Darren," I say "Am I losing my mind?"

"Baby no. It was just a dream."

"Dreams don't hurt, Darren."

I looked down at my arms in disbelief. There was nothing but soft, brown, unblemished skin.

Darren put his arms around my waist and pulled me close; He kissed the back of my neck. His warm lips on my skin were a welcome distraction from the winter chill. So, I closed the window and turned to face my love with a kiss. Our lips met passionately, and when we finally paused for a breath, I opened my eyes, looked into his face, and instead saw my sister.

I.

Another cold morning in Zion, Illinois.

Darren had just finished packing the rest of his clothes for his business trip. The scars on his face and neck were still healing.

I fucked up. I knew that. I didn't know what else to say except—

"Baby, Darren baby, I'm . . ."

"Sorry?" he started. "Yeah I know. But, tell me something I don't know. Like, what about my fucking face!"

He slammed his suitcase shut and began to work on the zippers and locks frantically. I tried to fight back the tears but they kept pouring out of my eyes.

"Darren, it was that damn dream. It seemed so real. I don't know how else to put it. She was real and then she was you!"

"Charlotte." Darren took a deep breath and exhaled my name slowly.

"Charlotte," he said. "You were right. You are crazy and you need help."

"I need you!" I reached out for him desperately and he recoiled like my touch was acidic to him. We had never fought like this before. Never.

"Don't leave me like this Darren."

"Charlotte, while I'm gone, get some help".

"But, we just—"

"*We* are okay. Just get help."

Sometimes I take long walks alone, and just breathe the air of my surroundings. And no matter how fair or foul the smell, the walk makes me feel centered, alive, and sane even. Today the walk didn't help. No matter what, I knew I would have to face an empty home.

My name is Charlotte Jackson. I think I am losing my mind.

II.

"What is your name?"

"Charlotte Jackson."

"Why are you here?"

"I don't know."

Dr. Corningstone, my shrink, was an astute, professional, shrew of a woman, whose bedside manner was burning the very fabric of my last nerve. She wore a lot of pink on her pale white cheeks. Her silvery hair was feathered as high as the sun. Her overall fashion sense was atrocious, but, at least, she took my insurance.

After a moment of listening to her pen scratch on her notepad, I decided to speak up again.

"That's not true."

"What?"

"I know why I am here."

She scratched on her pad some more and then said: "Please, continue".

I took a deep breath and then I spoke. I told her about my sister, the dreams, and the visions. I told her about Darren, and how I was afraid of losing him. By the time I was finished, I had broken down in chaotic sobs on her couch. She didn't seem too moved by my emotional breakdown, but I didn't know what else to say beyond boo-hoo. Except, "Dr. Corningstone, am I crazy?"

She only looked at me like she was staring into my head and trying to decipher the nuances of my brain.

"So, you have a sister?"

"No."

"But, you just said you had a sister and that you stole *her man* from her. Correct?"

"I don't know."

Dr. Corningstone pursed her lips together as her breath seeped through in an audible hiss. She tapped her pen three times on her notepad--tap, tap, and tap.

"Let me try something else," she said.

"Something what?"

"A different approach, I mean." Dr. Corningstone removed her glasses. "Tell me about your childhood, Charlotte."

"About what?"

"Your childhood, your years coming of age, and blossoming into a young woman, tell me about them." She spoke rather frankly and then added something rather startling. "Or can you?"

I thought real hard and tried to let my mind go back toward the past. I kept drawing a blank. There was something terrifying in those memories. Something even I didn't want to remember. But, if it meant that I could keep Darren, I thought I should at least be able to try.

"Doctor Corningstone, I can't remember anything." I spoke slowly as she handed me tissues. Her demeanor softened while I wept. I looked into her eyes and saw kindness.

"Mrs. Jackson, I may be able to help you. It is going to take time. But, you are going to have to learn how to trust. Do you trust me?"

"Yes," I said. "I think so."

"Good".

"Doctor Corningstone, what is wrong with me?"

"Well, in your short time on this couch, you have swung back and forth between two distinct personalities, and both of you claim to be Charlotte Jackson."

"Personalities? What am I to you, another Sybil?"

"It used to be called multiple personality disorder, now modern medicine identifies this condition as dissociative identity disorder or DID. I've never seen two personalities identify themselves with the same name. Honestly, your case is really unique to me."

"Unique?"

Dr. Corningstone continued to scratch on her note pad furiously.

"I think I'm going to be sick." I said as I tasted the bile rising in the back of my throat. This woman didn't give a damn about helping me. She just wanted her name in a medical journal.

"Dr. Corningstone, I will not be your guinea pig. I came to you for help."

"And Ms. Jackson, you will receive it. Now, if I still have your trust, you and I are going to work through this together."

III.

Dr. Corningstone fingered the silver filigree pin on the lapel of her navy striped blouse, and spoke carefully into the phone so that her assistant could hear her clearly. I felt like I was sitting on a mental and emotional powder keg. She told her assistant to clear her schedule for the rest of the day and had her set up a camcorder in the room.

"What the hell is the camera for?"

"Ms. Jackson, I need you to see what I am seeing."

"This *will* remain confidential, won't it?"

"Ms. Jackson, this *will* remain entirely between us."

"But—"

"You have my word."

I immediately thought of Darren. If therapy didn't work, I would have no one.

"Alright?" I said willingly. "What do I need to do?"

"Relax. Lie down. And breathe, Ms. Jackson." Dr. Corningstone's voice took on a soothing tone. It was almost motherly.

"My assistant will set up the camera and then we will begin."

IV.

"Charlotte, I want you to count backwards from ten with me, and when you reach one, you will be thirteen years old. Do you understand?"

"Yes."

"We will start now: 10 . . . 9 . . . 8 . . . 7 . . . 6 . . . 5 . . ."

Watching that tape afterwards was like having an out of body experience. I could see myself dressed plainly in denim jeans and printed long sleeved tee, brown boots, afro puffed high, and no makeup. I was beautiful.

"Where are we now Charlotte?" I could hear Dr. Corningstone speak, and see her sitting near the couch where I lay. She was still plain and garish in bold stripes, pink cheeks and white make up.

"NOGO."

"What is NOGO, Charlotte?"

"North Chicago."

"I see. Where are we at exactly?"

"We at my house. Upstairs. In my room."

I could see myself speaking, but hearing it made me shudder. I sounded just like a child while under hypnosis. I looked over at Dr. Corningstone. She just put her hand on my shoulder and bade me to continue to watch.

"What are you doing?"

"We kissing."

"Who are you kissing?"

"I don't want to say."

"It's alright. We are safe here, Charlotte. Now, who are you kissing?"

"My boyfriend."

"Go on, Charlotte."

"We on the bed. He stops. He looking at me like he scared. He say somebody coming. He ask if I locked the door."

"Did you lock the door, Charlotte?"

"I don't know."

I could see myself breathing faster, and the childlike voice that was escaping my lips grew more frantic.

"What's happening now?" said Dr. Corningstone.

"Oh God. The door is opening."

"Who's there, Charlotte?"

Watching those voices come out of me felt so unreal. I shook my head and covered my eyes, but Dr. Corningstone tapped my shoulder, and bade me to keep looking.

"She see us."

"Who's at the door Charlotte?"

"Chuck! Chuck! Chuck!"

"Charlotte, who's there?"

"I'm going to tell my momma!"

"Charlotte! Who's going to tell momma?"

"Gaylord! Gaylord!"

"Who is saying that, Charlotte?"

"She is. She gone tell Momma!"

"Who is she, Charlotte?

"You a fag Chuck!"

"No! I don't want to be!"

"You is, you is, you is, ha!"

"Please don't tell momma!"

"I'm gonna."

"You tell momma, I kill you."

"Kill who, Charlotte? Who is going to tell Momma?"

"I am!"

"Who are you?"

"I am Charlotte Jackson!"

"Who are you going to kill?"

"Chuck."

*"**Why**?"*

"Chuck pushed me down the stairs, and I hit my head real hard."

"Why did Chuck push you down the stairs?"

"Because he a Gaylord and he didn't want me to tell momma."

V.

"Alright, Charlotte Jackson, just breathe."
When I came to, I was sobbing with my head on Dr. Corningstone's shoulder. Then I saw the video and I finally remembered everything. I didn't mean to hurt Charlotte. I didn't mean to make my mother cry.
When they buried my sister, Charlotte, they couldn't prove her death as anything else but an accident. I guess it's just as well. When momma died, she never knew the truth. I never had the opportunity to come out to her and tell her who I really was. After I graduated from college and found work, I was out and proud and living my life. I thought after the operation I wouldn't need to live in hiding or shame anymore. And for a time, I felt completely liberated on my own. Then, I met a man named Darren, fell in love with him and after that, the nightmares began.

When I made it home, I disrobed, looked into my full length bathroom mirror, and stared at my nakedness. Tears still ran down my cheeks in huge mascara drips, and my hair was a mess. I realized that I would have to let Darren know everything, but first, in order to heal, I needed to look her in the eye and ask for forgiveness myself.

"Charlotte. Come to me, I know what I did. Charlotte, I know what I did to you. I was wrong."

The image in the mirror was no longer my own. My sister stood before me wearing my skin, my hair, my eyes, and no tears; nothing but a face of stone.

"Charlotte?"

She said nothing. She just stared at me like stone. And the look chilled me to the bone.

"Charlotte, I'm sorry. We were both young. We were both just children. But, you always fit in with the other kids, and you knew that I didn't."

"I always wanted to be like you, Charlotte. To be loved like you and be admired like you, it is all I ever wanted. I never wanted to take anything away from you. I never wanted to take your life. I just wanted you to see me and not be ashamed."

I could hear the emotion in my voice. I could feel my own heart breaking for my mom and my sister. I could still feel the tears roll hot down my face. But, that image in the mirror. She didn't even crack a smile.

"Charlotte, I've always liked boys, but more than that, I always wanted to be the girl I felt I was. But, things happened. Things happened that I can't take back. And now I'm here, and I can't say enough how much I want your forgiveness."

The image didn't move, the expression on the face never changed, but a single tear did roll down her cheek. And it was then that I knew she heard and understood me.

"I love you, Charlotte."

I reached out and touched the surface of the mirror, and she reached back to me with a look of frozen understanding. And for the first time in my life, I felt completely unafraid like this image before me wasn't a monster or a mistake. She was my sister and she was proud of me.

I collapsed with relief with my forehead against the mirror glass. I could feel Charlotte gently reaching for me and I like an idiot welcomed the embrace of my sister. I blacked out for a minute.

"Charlotte? Charlotte, I'm home."

I heard the voice of my love calling to me from the front room. I heard my voice speak from the other side of the mirror.

"I'm in the bathroom baby! I was about to take a shower. Care to join me?"

She smiled a vicious smile at me, licked her lips, and kissed the glass I was trapped in. I tried to scream, I tried to break the barrier. I wanted to scratch her eyes out. But, there was nothing I could do anymore. Miss 'Thing' was already in my body making love to Darren in the shower.

Author Interviews - Jacqueline Nicole Harris

Hi, Jacqueline Nicole Harris!

What was your inspiration for this story?
My main inspiration for this story was my younger self growing up in North Chicago, IL. Like my main character, Charlotte, I am a fraternal twin. Unlike Charlotte, I have never had issues with gender identity.

When we were younger, my brother and I were often at odds like most siblings are. It seemed like he was the popular one and I was not. I got bullied a lot. I had body image issues and often times I wished I had had a sister my age that I could talk too about those things.

Anyway, Charlotte is a lot like me. She wants to live life on her own terms. Charlotte just wants to be Charlotte and happy--if that makes any sense.

I can only imagine what it is like to be LGBT and young. You've got the world all around you telling you to live and behave one way and then you have the yearnings of your own heart. Everyone wants to be accepted for who they feel that they are, and even as a grown-up, straight, black female, I still don't always feel comfortable in my own skin.

Why did you choose a Black woman as your main character?
I chose a transgender female for my main character, because that is direction the story dictated that I go in. When I begin to write my stories, I don't necessarily think about black or white, male or female. The plot itself is like an unformed lump of clay in my head.

Once I have a plot, I need a setting. Then I keep writing and inwardly I begin to ask myself questions, and a character sketch forms:

Who is she? Her name is Charlotte.

What is her problem? Charlotte thinks she is losing her mind.

Why? She really doesn't know, but it has something to do with her sister.

The story itself went through quite a few changes. Charlotte was at first a full grown female, with a supernatural doppelganger that was trying to take over her life. That has been done so much before. Usually the spirit double is just plain evil for no reason. That is bland storytelling, in my opinion.

In the end, I wanted to tell a story of regret and revenge; with shock and awe. Some supernatural stories have plots where things happen for no reason and the story works. I just couldn't do that. It didn't make sense to me to write "Sisters" that way, and truthfully, I'd still probably be writing it if I had gone my original route.

Why did you want to submit to Black Girl Magic Lit Mag?
I have been rejected by the best, but I haven't had my writings rejected by my own. I like what this magazine represents and after writing and performing poetry for so long, I took a chance.

And I am glad I took that chance. Acceptance or not, Black Girl Magic Lit Magazine is necessary and I am proud to be a part of it.

What are your favorite novels or short stories?
My desert island top 5 novels or short stories and why:
5. 1408 (not the movie) from Everything's Eventual by Stephen King. This story is terrifying and a lot of fun to read. You know that person in the movie theater who won't stop talking at the screen? That is the way I am with 1408 and all the stories in Everything's Eventual. Call me crazy, but I love it.
4. Really, Really, Really Weird Stories by John Shirley. Somethings you have to read over and over again just to get it. And I love a challenge. And just like the title to this collection, I'm really weird.

3. Fledgling by Octavia Butler. I discovered the writings of Octavia Butler after she had passed away in 2005. And I love vampire fiction, and Fledgling is a gem to have in my collection.

2. Heaven to Hell by Langston Hughes. I have a collection of short stories by the Harlem Renaissance poet and Heaven to Hell is one of the best flash fiction pieces I have ever read. Very funny. It is about a woman who is gone to Heaven with her husband, only to see that the other woman has also made it up to the pearly gates as well.

1. Twisted Tales by Brandon Massey. Nothing better than when a man can write strong female characters. In Twisted Tales, the story "Predators", is one of my absolute favorites of his. Brandon Massey is the bomb and has written some very scary tales. Check him out whenever, you won't be disappointed.

Tell us something about your future writing endeavors?
Currently I am working on my first novel. I set a deadline for it that I may never reach, but that remains to be seen.
I'm always writing poetry and from time to time I blog. The deadline for the novel is December 2016. The working title is Good Hair, Bad Magic.

Thanks for your submission. Where can we find you on Social Media?
www.facebook.com/PoeticJNHarris
poeticjharris.wordpress.com
@PoeticJHarris

The Souvenir - Jacqueline Nicole Harris

Douglas Richter liked living alone. He never asked for much from the universe except for complete isolation and independence. Of the few talents he had the one true gift the Lord had given him was the one that got him into the most trouble. It also paid the majority of his bills. Douglas Richter was given a rather strange ability in the realm of psychics and palm readers.

Douglas was highly empathic. He had the rare ability of extreme retro-cognition. He could touch no one. He could touch nothing without drawing all their energy completely into himself. Among things that were extraordinary or supernatural, Douglas was a much sought after statistical anomaly, and for a price, Douglas Richter could reveal all things to anyone.

But, it was always for a price. You see, Douglas was a person who valued his privacy more than anything else. He paid for that privacy on a constant basis. At his mansion, security systems, trained attack dogs, and ex-military personnel were all at his beck and call twenty-four hours a day.

Douglas was a vegan. He made his own meals from food he grew himself every day. Not, that he didn't like meat. He just couldn't touch it without feeling and reliving the creature's last moments. He could only vaguely recall what his mother's hamburgers tasted like. No flesh had touched his hand or lips in years.

Douglas wore the same dark clothes all the time. Only natural fibers, like cotton, could touch his skin. And then, there were the gloves. The gloves were the final word to his attire. They had belonged to his father and were made of white linen. His father had died peacefully in his sleep when Douglas was eighteen.

Douglas Richter looked at his cursed blessing as just something to endure for the benefit of others. He tried to keep a positive attitude in most things. He lived a laugh and the world laughs with you style mantra. He would receive letters from all other world asking for help in kidnapping cases, unsolved murders, and disappearances. Generally, he could solve a problem from the comfort of his home sometimes by touching the letter and then returning the answer to the sender. Douglas was that good.

So, when the letter from Mamie Burton came to his fortress of solitude, Douglas was shocked when he took off his gloves and could feel nothing at all.

Dear MR. Richter:

My name is Mary Agnes "Mamie" Burton, and I need your help. I am a very old woman, and my time is short. I want to remember something. Something painful I had forgotten a long time ago. I believe that the answer sits in front of me as I type this letter. I know that it is rare for you to make personal visits, but you are more than welcome in my home if you can help me remember why I held on to this thing in a jar. I am willing and able to pay you anything. I cannot send this item to you. I can only wait for your reply.

My sincerest wishes to you Mr. Richter,
Mamie Burton

Douglas was intrigued and more than a little terrified. Though, there was nothing visually odd about the letter. It just felt impersonal; like an extremely powerful third entity might be drawing his power away. He dropped the letter and let it float clumsily to the floor by his feet. He reached for the envelope, felt the same draw and saw the same blank in his mind.

"Mamie Burton must be no dummy," he thought to himself. "She had clearly done some research and put some thought into this. I can't feel a thing."

Douglas looked at the return address: 606 Elm Street, Newport, Arkansas.

Douglas decided he would go to Mamie Burton's home.

"It is a pleasure to finally meet you, Mr. Richter." Mamie Burton opened the porch screen door and gingerly stepped aside to let Douglas Richter in her home. She would not touch him. His letter to her had said not to touch him. He wore dark clothing and white linen gloves, which was odd to her, since it was mid-July in Arkansas.

The air-conditioning in the humble Burton abode was on full blast. Douglas breathed in the cool air and exhaled a sigh of relief before seating himself on the couch.

"Would you like some lemonade, Mr. Richter," said Mamie. "I made it fresh this morning."

"No, thank you. Remember, I cannot touch anything." Douglas Richter didn't look at the old black woman directly. His eyes seem to flit about like he was studying the room.

Three or four quick steps into the kitchen and Mamie Burton was back with a pitcher of lemonade and tea cakes. She had also made a glass for herself. Gingerly, she set an empty glass and the china dish with the tea cakes in it on the glass coffee table next to Richter. Then, she sat down in the recliner across the room from him.

"You have a nice home Mrs. Burton.," said Douglas with a forced smile.

"Thank you," she said.

"I am sorry, Ms. Burton, but I cannot eat those cookies," Douglas said while gesturing at the tea cakes.

"I am sure you went through a lot of trouble to make them."

"No trouble, Mr. Richter, no trouble at all", she said and smiled.

Mamie Burton had a kind face and a nice smile, Douglas thought to himself. She could not have possibly meant any harm to him. But, the nature of that curious letter was on his mind. How could anyone send something and he not feel anything but paper on his fingertips?

"I know what you are thinking," said Mamie. "They all think it when they meet me."

"Think what?" said Douglas sounding incredulous.

"You think that I am strange," said Mamie with a matter of fact tone, but not harshly.

"Whatever do you mean?" said Douglas.

"I didn't physically write the letter, Mr. Richter." said Mamie.

"You didn't write the letter?" said Douglas. "Well, then who did?"

Mamie's Mona Lisa smile never left her face, but she could see she was starting to bother her guest. She felt it would be rude to keep him in suspense. Still, this was the most fun messing with somebody she had ever had in years.

"I wrote the letter with my mind, Mr. Richter. You know, mentally." Mamie thought he would get it by then. But, the young still have a long way to go before they catch up with the old.

"I am afraid that I don't know, Mrs. Burton, what you are talking about." Douglas could hear his voice starting to rise with anger. Was this elderly woman playing mind games with him? Did he actually step into this with a clear head?

"Mr. Richter," started Mamie", Psychics, palm readers, and even those such as yourself, come a dime a dozen from era to era. But, I am something totally different. I can see into people's heads and move objects without touching them. I am of a rare breed."

"You are completely out of your mind, and so am I for coming here." spat Douglas.

"If you don't believe me, just watch those tea cakes."
Mamie was used to non-believers. She was also used to
converting them, too. Her mind flexed like a bicep and many
ridges and wrinkles appeared on her forehead, but, as soon as
this was accomplished, the tea cakes began to fly in all
directions around the room. Then, to accentuate her point,
Mamie made the tea cakes float a circle around Douglas's head.

"Ok," said Douglas, "You've made your point"."

"Eat a tea cake, Mr. Richter. They are very nice," said
Mamie. She waved her hand and three tea cakes floated back
onto the plate while one landed in Douglas's lap.

Douglas said nothing and felt nothing as he reached for
the cookie and placed it carefully back onto the plate.

"I am not here for games, Mamie Burton.," snapped
Douglas. "This was not a pleasure trip for me. It is always
dangerous for me and everyone around me when I leave my
home. There are things about *my gifts* I don't know, things I
can't control. So, if you are through wasting my time with
parlor tricks, we can continue onward to the business at hand.
Or, I can leave."

"Mr. Richter", started Mamie. "I beg of you to stay. It
has been so long since I have had any real company. And, I
really do need your help.""

Richter couldn't leave her, though he had come close to
wanting to leave. Something about this woman reminded him
of his own mother. Also, Douglas had never met anyone close
to being his equal in any way. Without saying another
disparaging word, Douglas picked up a tea cake and took a bite.

"These are delicious, Ms. Burton," said Douglas after he
had swallowed the last of it.

"Thank you, Mr. Richter," said Mamie.

They talked for a long time. Mamie Burton had done her
research on the young man. She didn't speak of this. Instead,
Mamie Burton talked mostly about her life in the South and
how she never quite fit in with her peers in school. She had
lived through so much.

Douglas listened intently to her. He still wasn't sure what he was getting himself into. But, the more she spoke, the more he began to glimpse at the historical as well as the personal significance of his purpose that day.

"You marched with Dr. King?" Douglas asked incredulously at one point.

"Right through Selma, Alabama!" She snapped. "And I was arrested with him, too."

"Wow," Douglas said with a smile. "You are living, breathing piece of history."

"I wished others felt that way today. To the youth around here, I am mostly just the weird old lady who lives down the street that nobody talks too," said Mamie Burton. "The younger children actually believe my house is haunted."

Then her countenance grew a bit sullener, bitter even.

"Mr. Richter, you are right to live alone as you do. I know you wonder what it is like to be around others and wonder what life would be like without your particular talents. But, if I could choose a whole another life, I would choose yours. It is hard to live amongst regular folks, who take life for granted, and believe in nothing but what they see flashing on an electronic screen or something they heard about from some old book long time ago. We live on the fringe of things seen and unseen. No one but us can know what that's like."

"No one has ever said that to me before," thought Douglas to himself. Though he did not say that aloud, she knew he thought it.

Instinctively, he felt like hugging this old woman whom he'd only just met. But, he then remembered the danger. Still, no one had ever understood what it was like to be him before, and now there was this wonderful wise person in front of him and he could not even shake her hand. Pity.

"I am scared, Mr. Richter," Mamie Burton said softly.

"Scared of what?" said Douglas.

"The reason why I brought you here today", she paused as she slowly became emotional. "The reason . . . I can't bring myself to go to the police with this. It would destroy too many people's lives."

"This is about the 'thing in a jar', isn't it?"" Douglas said.

"Yes."

"Do you want me to look at it?" asked Douglas.

"No, I need you to touch it," said Mamie.

"What is accomplished if I touch it, Mamie? What is all this about?" Douglas was growing confused at the sudden emotional change in Ms. Burton. It worried him.

"When I was about ten years old, I started sneak out of the house at night. Just little trips here and there. I didn't mean any harm, I just always thought about the world outside of Newport. I had a wanderlust inside of me, Mr. Richter. I hated it here. The way people were back then to one another was horrible."

"Go on", said Douglas.

"Well, many of my classmates can tell you now, if they are still living, that there was no reason for any Negro child to be wandering around at night in the South", said Mamie. "Those were dangerous times."

"I don't understand," said Douglas.

Mamie took a deep breath and when she exhaled she continued. Her face was like stone.

"Lynchings, Mr. Richter, were a part of life. Many black men and women, but especially our men, were murdered hideously in cold blood by mobs of angry whites. My brother was one of those who never made it to see desegregation or a Black President."

Mamie continued, "My family was poor. We couldn't afford a burial, but that didn't matter since we had 'no' body to bury. I haven't spoken his name in years, but my brother's name was Cloise and he was my best friend."

"I couldn't do anything, but watch as my mother slowly work herself to death with grief, while my father grew cold and distant. I couldn't do anything, Mr. Richter, but watch and remember, watch and remember. But, now my time is short and my memory is leaving me. I have been diagnosed with Alzheimer's, Mr. Richter. It is a fact that people like us use more than ten percent of our mental capacities. So, it is likely that we, you and I, are more susceptible to the disease. The medicine I take helps keep me lucid. Anyhow, I have a cleaning job with a wealthy family that used to employ my mother in the old days. My brother and I would even sometimes play with their children when it was allowed or no one was watching. They were planning some renovations for the attic space at the mansion and I was head of the cleanup crew. And that is when I came across some old pictures and the jar."

Douglas was already drawing pictures in his mind of what was to come. He came up with some pretty wild scenarios, but nothing was solid as it was not his talent to make predictions.

"You took these items from your employers without their knowledge," said Douglas.

"Yes, I did Mr. Richter." She knew that she had broken the law. Douglas could see no fear in her eyes however.

"Mr. Richter, you have come all this way, would you like to see what I found?"

Douglas said nothing, but gently nodded his head in affirmation.

"Ok then, I will bring them out." Mamie slowly got up and, then with two, three quick steps, she disappeared into the back of the house.

While she was gone, Douglas pondered over the significance of the photos and why she had left that particular detail out of her letter. He imagined that the photos must hold some clue as to what was in the jar itself.

But, if that was the case, she could have sent the photos through the mail instead of that damnable letter. Something was amiss, but he had gone too far to back out now.

Besides, if this were a trap, he could be putting himself and the old woman at risk. But, why would she go all this way to trap him?

Douglas did not have long to sit and wonder. With two, three quick steps, Mamie had returned with a silver platter. On said platter was an envelope and the jar.

"I can't touch that," thought Douglas suddenly. "I won't."

"You will," said Mamie Agnes. "Because you are under my power and have been since you received my letter, Mr. Richter.'"

Douglas caught a glimpse of his own reflection in the shiny silver platter. The flesh of his lips had folded inward into a thin black line that was slowly disappearing seamlessly into his face. Douglas could not even scream.

"I can do the same thing to your nose," said Mamie Agnes. "I can seal it shut. Then you'll really be up shit creek!"

Douglas thought he had no one to blame but himself. He would have never allowed himself to get personally involved in a case. And he should have never left the comfort of his home for this old bitch.

"I heard that, Mr. Richter." Mamie chuckled defiantly. And then she added with a snort: "I don't have Alzheimer's disease, Mr. Richter. I remember damn well what happened to my brother Cloise, and all those who were responsible for his untimely demise because I witnessed it myself! I never marched with Dr. King, and frankly my dear, I could give a damn if we ever all just got along."

"Why are you doing this to me," thought Douglas. "What do you get out of this, some kind of paranormal superiority? I had nothing to do with the death of your brother!'"

"No, you were conceived after your mother had *your* brother aborted," said Mamie. "Maybe, she should have aborted you too!"

"What are you saying?" Douglas was slowly getting the hang of telepathy. His words were coming in like screams in Mamie Agnes's mind. Still, she was like a stone; completely unmoved and unimpressed.

"Touch the jar, Mr. Richter," said Mamie. "Take off those stupid linen gloves, reach out, and touch the jar. I promise, if you survive the experience, all will be revealed. No hair off my ass, if you don't. It is just like you thought, you never should have come here."

"And if I don't?" thought Douglas.

"If you don't, well then, you aren't the first man I've killed,"" she chuckled. "You will be the last, however."

"No!" Douglas thought. He tried to fight the compulsion to obey her commands, but the more he resisted the stronger she became.

"No?" Mamie laughed. "Ha! You will touch the jar Douglas or I will do to you what I did to the entire Mason-Richter family, babies and all! Touch it! Touch the jar, and know the truth!"

Douglas robotically removed one glove and began to reach for the jar. When the skin on the tips of his fingers made contact with the rim of the lid, inside of his mind, Douglas screamed in mortal terror. His eyes became white as snow.

"Do you see it? Do you? Can you feel what they did to your father?" Mamie's voice flooded over his mental screams like peels of thunder.

Douglas saw an image of his own mother. She was 18 years old and clearly with child. Even in the glow of the mob's torches, her face was clearly streaked with tears, while the white faces of men, women, and children were twisted with glee and hatred.

Douglas could taste the hot salt of blood erupting from Cloise's lips and he could hear the laughter of the mob as Cloise pleaded for mercy from the Lord. The mob showed no mercy. They took turns whipping him with belts, barber straps, and horse whips, and when he was too weak to scream anymore, they through rock salt in the wounds. A rusty razorblade was used to cut off his fingers, his toes, but ultimately, it was the man that Douglas had called dad all of his life, the one who had died peacefully in his sleep dreaming of the love he had for his gifted white son, who removed Cloise Burton's genitalia and kept it as a souvenir in a pickle jar.

In shock, and bleeding profusely, Cloise Burton was ultimately burned to death. There would be no physical evidence left in the morning. In death, Cloise managed to focus on his sister, Mary Agnes, who had hidden in the thorns of a briar patch with her hands over her mouth to silence her screams.

In the mirror of her mind's eye, Mamie had always been the little girl hiding in that thorny bush, utterly consumed with contempt for what had pasted for Southern justice. Cloise had loved the white woman that was Douglas's mother and she loved Cloise. When she had been raped by Douglas's 'dad', she had aborted that child. But when she and Cloise made love and conceived Douglas, they were going to run away together. They never made it out of town. Together anyway.

Mamie moved the jar away from Douglas's hand with her mind. Douglas's eyes never went back to their normal brown. They stayed white.

"What's wrong boy," she said. "You look like you've just seen a ghost."

"Aggy May?" Douglas's voice was not his own. Douglas wasn't there anymore. "Aggy May? Is that you talking? I can't see."

"Cloise!" Mamie Burton jumped in terror.

"Aggy May?" Cloise said. "Where am I? I was happy. I was with Elizabeth. I was waiting for you. Been waiting for you forever.""

"Cloise", started Mamie, "I don't understand. Where were you waiting for me at?"

"Heaven," said Cloise. "It is so beautiful. And God is all around, he heard me call. Can't you hear Him?"

Mamie Burton was dumb struck.

"No, bruh. I can't hear Him," she said. "I don't want to hear anything from Him. He let them take you away from me."

"Aggy May," said Cloise. She didn't answer. Cloise heard the sound of glass breaking. It was the jar.

"Aggy May," said Cloise. "Please talk to me. Where am I? I want to go home."

Mary Agnes pressed a shard of broken glass to her throat with her right hand.

"Cloise, I missed you so much", she sobbed. "And I am so sorry, but you've got a new body, a second chance at life. And I am so tired."

"Aggy May," said Cloise. "I want to go home."

"Good bye, Cloise", she said.

Douglas Richter was institutionalized by court order when no evidence was found that made him completely culpable in Mary Agnes Burton's death. To this day, he still insists that his name is Cloise Burton.

And he still wants to go home.

From Peter - Nicky Nicholson-Klingerman

Being a lesbian is not as exciting as you would think. It's not all pride parades, gay bars and watching *Ellen,* especially relationships. For the most part, it's as boringly normal as any of the other heterosexual ones. It definitely feel like it's fifty percent housework - and twenty-five percent of that is arguing over whose turn it is to do the dishes since neither of us is Type A enough to put up a schedule - the other fifty percent is spent playing board games while watching Netflix.

I tell Mama this as we prepare dinner and she just sucks her teeth. "It's not normal what God meant between a man and a woman to be between two women," she tells me in her lilting, leftover Caribbean accent. My mother lived all over the Caribbean - Jamaica, Barbados, the Virgin Islands, etc. - because of her father's tour boat business. Since she lived half her life on the ocean her accent never really landed on any particular island.

I let her comment roll off my back with a quiet "Mmm" as I chopped up vegetables for our Sunday dinner. My friends never really understood why I put up with my mother's views on my "lifestyle". I suppose I was used to it by now. She was my mother and I loved her. Family stays with you when friends come and go, even if they stay with a permanent look of disapproval. Anyway, she was much better than she used to be. In fact, other than the odd comment about burning in hell and no grandchildren, we have a perfectly normal mother-daughter relationship. I put up with her homophobia much the way someone would put up with a loved one's shopping addiction or smoking. You tell them they should stop but you can't really abandon them.

I think I'm also protective of her. I don't want people to judge her so harshly. Besides being a brilliant accountant as well as the only black female one at her company, she volunteers her little free time to advise minority small business owners on how to manage their finances better. People, I've learned, are not two dimensional.

So instead of getting mad, I laugh and say, "As long as I got L, it doesn't matter to me how abnormal God or anyone else may think it is."

Mama purses her lips but she refuses to say anything bad about L. For all her displeasure at my sexuality, she adores L. Everyone does. L could walk into a room and be friends with everyone almost instantly. I, on the other hand, prefer nestling among the wallflowers or basking in the effervescent glow that surrounds L at all times.

For L's part, she also never really understood how I could deal with my mother sometimes. I tell that in comparison to her mom who attends Pride with us and has been in attendance since L came out in high school, my mom seems a little stiff. But for my mom, just telling me that it isn't normal rather than casting out my demons is about as accepting and tolerant as she will get. Fine by me, I'll take it.

However, L often says that in general I'm not really as pissed off about homophobia as I am about racism or sexism. I never let any racist comments go unnoticed. If you say "hit like a girl" I will probably demonstrate what that actually means. During movies or TV shows, I point out every smidgen of institutional racism and misandry. Don't get me wrong, I cheer every time a lesbian character is introduced. There are fingernail marks permanently scarred into L's arm when I grabbed her after Viola Davis was revealed to be bisexual in "How to Get Away with Murder". I rejoice for every beam that sheds light on the LGBTQA community but you can only fight so many battles. Racism and sexism are my go-tos and though I'll fight the occasional skirmish for LGBTQA issues, I'll be angry all the time if I take on one more thing.

"Mama, where's Daddy?" I ask her, hoping to change the subject.

"He's in the study and hasn't come out since this morning", she huffs. I smile. My dad was a writer and a very eccentric genius.

He must have heard because just then, he popped out of the study with a glazed look and running his hand through his perpetually tangled red hair. He always has the air of a bright red kite lazily trying to leave earth with Mama as the string that connects him to this realm and reality.

They met off the coast of Jamaica when he was visiting for a school trip his senior year of high school. My mother was running the boat tour and while she was talking about coral reefs and pointing out landmarks, he kept asking her about mermaids, fairies, and Anansi the spider. "You'd a thought they were real creatures the way he talked. So calm and serious. Almost had me believing mermaids were right beneath boat, just outta sight", Mama would laugh whenever she talked about it.

Somehow, he caught her attention and they met up every day until he left for home. They sent letters until finally she came over to the US to attend University of Miami to study finance. After helping her father run a pretty successful business, she already had the experience to become a level-headed accountant. Dad went to some hippie-dippie liberal arts college in the area, who were floored to have someone with a perfect SAT score and off-the-charts IQ. He didn't care about good schools or a prestigious reputation. He only cared about three things at the time - being close to his new girlfriend, finishing his first novel and discovering proof of any mythical creature - mermaid or otherwise.

Mama waves him into the kitchen and he shuffles over to us. "Hey, sweetheart, when did you get here?"

I lean over and give him a hug, "About an hour ago. How's the new book coming along?"

He tugs on his beard and looks vaguely out the kitchen window, "It's going pretty well. Finally decided on Captain Bell Hooks' demise." He was working on a philosophical book where some of the greatest writers and thinkers were stuck in Never Land.

Mama claps the sides of his face with her messy hands and kisses him with a big smack, "You work too hard. Go sit on the porch and talk with your daughter." Dad shrugs, looking at me.

I give her sidelong glance, wondering if this is her way of getting rid of me. We were just about to start on the beef patties and I wasn't that great at stuffing them. She always said I stuffed more in my mouth than in the pastries. "Alright, Mama, I'll get out of your hair for now", I sigh and splash water at her while I wash my hands.

She shrieks and shoos me out of the kitchen. "Get out of here girl! You'll mess up my hair." As there were beans and shredded lettuce already stuck to her curls, a little water probably would've helped.

Successfully shooed out of the house by my mother, dad and I settle ourselves on the old swing, rocking into a comfortable silence. If he cared about such things, my dad would probably be socially awkward but as he didn't, he went through life with an untroubled ease that made me jealous. He doesn't mind monopolizing conversations with things that only he would care about. What's more, he is so enthusiastic and brilliant, most people get so caught up and forget they aren't talking about the usual things like celebrities, politics or so-and-so's divorce. He lived in world of his own and withdrew from it only when my mother forced him to or to randomly say something profound.

Once in seventh grade, my math teacher suggested I get a tutor because of my constant questions. My dad calmly made the observation that as a teacher, it was her job to teach me math and since I had a solid B- in the class, perhaps her suggestion of a tutor was influenced by stereotypes and racism. Of course, she was offended and protested profusely but my dad cut in with a perfect lecture on a recent study that showed that everyone was influenced by racism, even the mixed black man who ran the study. He followed with another study on teachers administering discipline based on race and studies where little kids had to point to which black or white doll was the bad/ugly or good/pretty doll. She might have taken true offense then if he hadn't also mentioned how magical creatures were not safe from the Western world's whitewashing. This completely confused her and we left the parent-teacher conference with no plans of getting me a tutor.

Dad finally breaks the silence, "How's L doing in school?"

"Really great, she loves it. She'll be finished with her masters in Psychology next spring then she'll be able to start her residency at the clinic," I tell him. L has dreams of opening addiction clinic which I think is brilliant. With her ability to relate to anyone and make them feel comfortable, she makes the perfect counselor.

He nods, "That's good, I'm glad for her. Why isn't she here for dinner?"

I hesitate for a beat, then say, "She has a lot of studying to do. She hopes to be here next Sunday though."

Dad peers intently at me but doesn't say anything. I pull a splinter away from the ancient swing, trying to keep my face neutral. L loves my mom's spirit and my dad's eccentricity, she really did. But sometimes, they can be intense. She has a much harder time holding her temper when my mother makes a comment and my dad just looks away. So she comes when she can and lights up the room with her laughter, philosophical arguments, and bright eyes.

"How's the illustrating going?" he asks, breaking me away from my thoughts.

For the past five years, I have been trying to break into the children's illustration business with little to no luck. Finally, *finally*, I got a job at a small printing press doing some illustration but mostly administrative work. It paid very little but at least I got some experience in my field of choice. "I like my job, but I'm still waiting, ya know?"

He leans forward unbalancing the swing a little and gives me a small, quizzical smile, "Waiting for what exactly?"

I shrug, noncommittal, "My big break I guess".

Dad tugs absentmindedly on his beard, "You know, I think I could talk to my agent".

I shake my head, "No, Daddy, I have to do this on my own."

He held up hand, "You didn't let me finish. I need a good illustrator for the book I'm doing. I want it to be a pseudo-children's/adult book. I think some vibrant illustrations would do the trick of fusing the adult aspects of the book with the childlike whimsy very well."

I look out at the setting sun and Mama's huge garden falling into shadow, "Well...a graphic novel might work better than just some illustrations."

Dad's eyes actually lost some of their fogginess and lit up, "See - this is why we need to do this. You have some great ideas. You're young, you're an artist, and you're my daughter. This is perfect."

I sit back, a little stunned at his enthusiasm. I would have to seriously think about it, but the idea was already taking hold of my mind and spreading roots. "It's definitely an idea," I say slowly", I'd like to know more about the book..., but I think this might be a fun project."

Dad gives me a real, full on grin. It's brilliant enough to burn away the rest of the fog that usually surrounds him, "I really hope you agree. Let me know as soon as possible when you're sure."

I smile a little, shaking my head. Dad was a writer and I was an artist. It made sense that we would work on something together eventually, though I'd hoped to have made some progress on my own. The small printing press was great experience but perhaps this was the foot in the door I needed.

We went back to swinging lazily in silence, a light summer breeze bringing us the smell of mint and lavender from Mama's herb garden. Minutes stretched by. Through the screen door, I could hear Mama bustling around in the house. Dad and I watch the world turn golden, both of us lost in thought. There is a heaviness in the air, a low humming that almost felt...magical.

I do not know where it came from, whether it sprang from my dad's mind or it got stuck between dimensions, but the tiniest, most delicate fairy flew up from the sunflower patch in front of the house. We saw it at the same time, a bright flash leaving a shower of dust behind it. I jump up, gasping and eyes wider than ever. The fairy spirals high into the air, transparent wings twinkling in the sunlight. I watch, breathless and shaky, as it blends into the sun-burnt sky. For one unbelievable moment, the world feels unbalanced and raw, like everything around me is floating away but I am immovable and this moment is endless.

It flies higher and higher until it disappears out of sight and everything falls back into place with a dull thud. My lungs cry out for air and I take a deep breath. Slowly, I look back at my dad. He hadn't jumped out of the swing like I had but he was wearing a faraway, dazed look that mirrored how I felt.

"Was that a fairy?" I breathe.

Dad nods and begins to swing again. He stares out over the sunflower patch for long time. I am practicing how to breathe when he murmurs, "Some of them followed me here".

I stare at him, "What...from where?" I feel light and dizzy, like the magic in the air hadn't quite faded yet and was trapped inside my head.

He leans back, arms folded comfortably across his chest, and says very quietly, "From Never Land".

Author Interviews - Nicky Nicholson-Klingerrman

Hi, Nicky Nicholson-Klingerman!

What was your inspiration for this story?
This story started out as a musing about how "normal" being a lesbian is and progressed from there, fueled by my obsession with Neverland. My own family played a huge role and this story is the hardest to let people read because it hits so close to home. My family is amazing and they shape who I am as well as my writing.

Why did you choose a Black woman as your main character?
I am a black woman and it was insanely difficult to find stories that prominently featured characters who looked like me. My mother tried to make sure I had stories with black kids. There were only a few but she made sure I had them. My biggest goal as a writer is to create diverse stories.

Why did you want to submit to Black Girl Magic Lit Mag?
I love that there is a literary magazines that empowers black women.

What are your favorite novels or short stories?
I love anything by Tamora Pierce. Her stories were the first I read that had women warriors in them. I also love *Bronx Masquerade* by Nikki Grimes, *Gabi in Pieces* by Isabel Quintero and *Liar* by Justine Larbalestier.

Tell us something about your future writing endeavors?
I am currently writing a retelling of the Princess and the Pea with diverse characters. The Prince is actually a girl. She was disguised as a boy after her twin brother was killed since women couldn't inherit the throne. I've also sending out my first novel called Catching Moonlight which is about a Latina girl who finds out she's part mermaid.

Thanks for your submission. Where can we find you on Social Media?
twitter.com/Nickythewriter

Featured Creator - Sophia Chester

Our Featured Creator for this issue is Sophia Chester, the author of a new YA Sci-Fi book entitled, Cosmic Callisto Caprica & The Missing Rings Of Saturn.

Sophia Chester lives in Cambridge, Maryland with her Mom, step Dad, four siblings, her rowdy Teenage Mutant Ninja Turtle watching little nephew Lem and her cranky cat Neko. If she's not watching Sailor Moon and wondering why the bad guys can't attack the sailor scouts while there transforming. She's probably hunched over her laptop typing up another Sci-Fi story and asking herself why she decided to become a writer in the first place. Sophia currently works for the Maryland State Senate as a clerk. Sophia loves photography, going to church, spending way too much money in Wal-Mart (it's literally the only place to shop at in town.), sleeping, reading YA novels and over-analyzing children's cartoons to see if they have some sort of deeper meaning. Cosmic Callisto Caprica & The Missing Rings Of Saturn is her first novel.

So, what was your inspiration for your book?
It was winter of 2013. I was snowed in and I decided to binge watch BattleStar Galactica and Mad Men. While I was binge watching both of these shows on Netflix I was also nursing this messy story that I had put together during Nanowrimo. However the story was a mess and I was starting to worry that there was nothing I could do to save it. So I decided to ditch that story and write something else. I wasn't sure what I wanted to write about. I was really in a Sci-Fi mood after watching Battle Star Galactica. Yet I was also mesmerized by the beautiful gowns and lovely set pieces from the show Mad Men. I wasn't sure what I wanted to do. After sitting down and brainstorming for a few days I decided to combine both into one story. I was going to tell a story in space but give the characters a retro 1950's look.

What made you choose to write a book with a Black woman protagonist?
I can't remember reading a single book growing up where the main character actually looked like me. Especially if the book had some sort of fantasy setting to it. There was nothing more frustrating than having to project myself onto a main character with brown hair and green eyes. Even worse having to settle for little scraps stuck between the pages where the author might have one black female character who you see only one time and that's it. I knew that if I was going to write my own book my main character was going to be a black girl. I know that somewhere out there is a little black girl who feels the same way that I did. Who wants to read a book with a main character who looks like her who actually saves the day. I'm writing this for her.

How do you feel being a Black female creator?
I feel like the odds are already stacked against me. I know that reading stories with a male lead is the norm. I feel like the industry wants diverse stories as long as there told a certain way. As long as the main character is white yet the supporting cast of characters who don't do much of anything are diverse then it's OK. If the main character is a minority along with the supporting cast then that's too diverse. I feel like producing your own works on your is the best option.

Like I said I feel like the industry is really only interested in "diversity" as long as it's told though the example I just provided. So submitting your works only to have it thrown onto a slush pile and lost to the annexes of time is a futile effort. I feel like crowdfunding is the way to go. People need to provide the funds for the type of diverse projects that they want to see. I chose to crowdfund Cosmic Callisto Caprica & The Missing Rings of Saturn on both Kickstarter and Indiegogo. I wish I had more confidence in myself. I made a lot of mistakes because I felt like my project wasn't good enough to be kickstarted. So I took a year off and I re-launched Cosmic Callisto Caprica on Indiegogo. My Indiegogo crowdfund was far more successful because I learned from my mistakes with my Kickstarter.

What do you think POC creators need to succeed?
A strong social media presence. I feel like the internet and social media is creating a sort of renaissance for black creators. It's giving us the opportunity to connect with people who are hungry for diverse stories and cutting out the middle man. By middle man I mean the entertainment industry that dictates what projects are seen and which ones stay buried forever. Gone are the days of hoping that someone will write an article about you in the newspaper. You don't have to rely on people to get the word out for you and your project. You can do it yourself on the internet. Bypassing social media and the internet is absolutely foolish. You're missing out on gaining a huge audience by not tapping into it. I mean you don't need to have 1 million followers. If you only have 20 or 200 people following you that's OK. As long as you have someone following you and showing you an interest in your project anything is possible. You never know who might re-tweet, reblog, or share your project. That could literally be the different between achieving success or failure.

What was the easiest and hardest thing about getting your project going?

The easiest thing for me was mailing out my gifts to my crowdfunding backers. The hardest was having to edit my story.

Tell us something about your future projects.
Right now I'm working on the sequel to Cosmic Callisto Caprica & The Missing Rings Of Saturn. I'm also thinking about maybe doing another crowdfunding project to help bring this book to life.

What does Black Girl Magic Mean to you?
For me it means to love everything that's magical about you. Whether it's your fluffy afro that reaches up to the sky or your two packs of Remy Brazilian hair that you bought at the corner store. It's loving the skin that you're in wither your dark, light or in between. It means loving your body unconditionally no matter how big or small certain parts are. It's just a way to appreciate the magic that's inside of you.

Where can we find you on Social Media?
https://www.facebook.com/CosmicCallistoCaprica/
http://sophiaslittleblog.tumblr.com/
https://twitter.com/SophiaTheAuthor
https://www.youtube.com/channel/UC_6nDqaSmBNW3_RmQ AM0ofQ

About Cosmic Callisto Caprica & The Missing Rings of Saturn

On the night of her high school graduation, an aspiring space detective, Cosmic Callisto Caprica, Cosmo to her friends, received an incredible gift from a well-respected senator - a trip on board the Titan, a luxury spaceship. Cosmo is incredibly excited to meet the beautiful yet controversial Martian Princess Rhea, one of Cosmo's heroes, and see the priceless Rings of Saturn on display in a jewelry showcase.

Cosmo and her childhood Martian nanny, Wendy, set off in the senator's spacecraft for what should be the journey of a lifetime.
But things go horribly wrong. Rampant discrimination. The disappearance of Wendy, along with nearly all the other Martian women on the Titan. And the theft of the Rings of Saturn all result in a mystery of historical proportions.

Cosmo goes undercover to find Wendy and the rings. But will she uncover the mystery before her cover is blown? Or will Cosmo be captured along with the other women, leaving the Rings of Saturn lost forever?

Join the fearless Cosmo in this fun and exciting futuristic mystery adventure — Cosmic Callisto Caprica and the Missing Rings of Saturn, by acclaimed author Sophia Chester

THANK YOU FOR YOUR SUPPORT

If you'd like to be the first to learn about Black Girl Magic Lit Mag news you can join our Mailing List at https://tinyletter.com/blackgirlmagicmag

You can also read story excerpts and read book reviews on our site at http://www.blackgirlmagicmag.com

We accept story submissions on a quarterly basis. If you're interested in submitting please check our website for guidelines.

We'd also love to connect with you on Twitter & Facebook.